A BOOK
ABOUT MY
MOTHER

———————

Toby Talbot

A BOOK

ABOUT MY

MOTHER

Farrar, Straus and Giroux

NEW YORK

Copyright © 1980 by Toby Talbot
All rights reserved
Published simultaneously in Canada
by McGraw-Hill Ryerson Ltd., Toronto
Printed in the United States of America
Designed by Cynthia Krupat
First edition, 1980
Library of Congress Cataloging in Publication Data
Talbot, Toby. / A book about my mother.
I. Title.
CT275.T7175T34   1980   974.7'042'0924 [B]   80–10973

For

Bella Tolpen

1904 – 1978

———————

En los brazos te tengo,
y me da espanto.
¿Qué será de ti, niño,
si yo te falto?

In my arms I hold you,
and I am afraid.
What will befall you, child,
if I am gone?

A SPANISH LULLABY

Oh, that my head were waters,
mine eyes a fountain of tears.

JEREMIAH

A BOOK
ABOUT MY
MOTHER

———————

There was a woman. A plain woman. That woman is no more.

My mother's time was up, they say. Dead and buried, she would say.

Her name was Bella Tolpen.

She had black hair. Pure black. Black as a gypsy's, glossy as a beetle's wing, and when struck by light, it flashed blue. As far back as my memory goes, she wore it short, letting it wave around the shape of her head in its own way. It never turned gray, but in her sixties passed from black to white. From jet to silver. From coal to ash.

Her eyes were dark brown, her lashes very straight and not long. The eyes and hair were what people remembered. Eyes that were expressive, playful, shrewd at times, soft and deep other times. She laughed easily. Was seventy-four when she died.

I kneel and tamp down the earth. Hardened February soil which has been loosened and dug deep to receive her body. Our first planting of spring. A soft snow falls, light and lacy as a bridal veil. As the veil that draped her in the wedding picture which still hangs over their empty bed. In that now unoccupied room. The white gauze this morning falls upon all of us—her survivors, the gravediggers, the rabbi. The earth is now my parents' bed. My father lay down before her and for four years waited in the darkness, through a long eternal night, to be joined by his mate. "It's so hard to sleep alone," he used to say. Mornings, when he awoke, his hand would reach out for hers. Now she joins him. The final tryst. It snows. It snowed all of yesterday but never emptied the sky. The snow is like feathers falling from goose-down pillows, like those we used to restuff together every few years in the bathtub when I was a child. The light is diffuse and hueless. I tamp down the soil, inhale the smell of loam. First we make mud pies, then sand castles, then gardens, then graves.

February soil webs my fingers. No new seed has gone in yet. Not even peas, or lettuce. Too early. My mother is of the earth now. That-is-where-she-is. Everything that I can ever hope to plant springs from her fertility. Tiny roots bursting from their pods and groping toward her nurture. Today the earth, pensive and in repose, receives its child in swaddling folds of white. Festoons of bridal snow. Baptismal shrouds. Nina, our eldest daughter, lays white gladiola on my mother's grave. Emily, our second-born, reads a poem she has written. Sarah, our youngest, looks on, pale and stunned. My sister and her family bow their heads to the rabbi's prayers. Softly the snow keeps falling, falling in thick drifts on my father's headstone, on the vines, on the iron grating, on the voices and words.

W e were supposed to go to Seville, my husband and I. The day before our departure I called her, one of those usual calls to say, Good morning, how did you sleep? How do you feel? The sort of call you make as the years go by and you become your mother's mother. She lived alone. So I repeated, "How do you feel?"

Oh, she told me, one day good and one day less good. The closest she ever came to complaint. Her remark triggered off my concern, for her sleep had been restless that past weekend and she'd mentioned a slight pain in her upper arm. A touch of flu, she'd conjectured, and had remained indoors. The ambiguity of her telephone reply, her indisposed weekend, the blizzard outside, and the imminence of our trip prompted me to say, "Mother, since we're going away tomorrow, I'd feel much better if the doctor looked at you. You've been a bit under the weather the last few days and there's no harm in getting a checkup . . ." I went on in that vein, pressing, in anticipation of the usual objections she put forth when it came to consulting doctors. She had small belief in medicine. I needn't have urged. She agreed. I made arrangements for Sarah, home from school due to blizzard shutdowns, to accompany her in a cab to New York Hospital, where her doctor was doing his morning rounds. Reassured, I proceeded to the university where

I teach, for the last class before intersession, mentally drawing up a list of what had to be packed for Seville. That was on Tuesday.

We postponed our trip. The doctor detected a slight pulmonary congestion, nothing to worry about, he assured us, but it would be best, he thought, for her to remain a few days in the hospital till the congestion cleared. At first, she told us, "Go. I don't want to spoil your trip. I'll be all right." But then she said, "Maybe you'd better stay." I'd already canceled our reservations.

On that last day, Saturday, my husband and I visited her. New York Hospital, a place that held traumatic memories: a child's crushed finger, a swallowed fishbone, a father undergoing exploratory abdominal surgery. My mother was in the Intensive Care Unit, where she'd been transferred two days earlier following an episode of heart failure. It was three in the afternoon. Nina was with her. Had been there on and off all day. Before we could even enter, the floor doctor informed us that the patient ought to rest, why didn't we go out and have some coffee? I didn't want to leave. Was angry to be kept from her—she didn't even know that I was in the corridor. But I went. We sat in the corner Greek luncheonette, drinking bitter, overcooked coffee. Nina ate a corn muffin, her breakfast and lunch.

"Bella will get better, I know she will," she argued, convinced that, if she persuaded us, her omnipotent parents, the outcome would be assured. "She's a tough lady, you know," Nina went on, her chin jutting forth emphatically. "Why, she even convinced the nurses this morning to allow her off the bed so that she could sit in a chair for a while." The coffee soured in my stomach as I thought of the beginning bedsores I'd noticed yesterday on my mother's left side, the result of five days of continually lying in bed. "Do you understand?" my daughter insisted. "She's going to get better!"

Back at the hospital, we were told that my mother was sleeping. We sat in the waiting room, we sat and sat, a captive audience to the conversation of another visiting family. Their relentless talk grated on my nerves. I moved into the corridor, waiting for my mother to awaken, reminding the apple-cheeked nurse on duty, by my conspicuous pacing and glances, of my presence. Green-coated hospital orderlies and nurse's aides, metal meal wagons, glided by noiselessly on the rubber-tiled corridor.

Shortly before six, my mother awoke.

"Only two can go in," said the nurse.

"Let me say good night," my daughter begged. She and I went in together. My husband remained outside. We passed the battery of machines that recorded the life functions of the six patients in the unit. My mother was resting against a mound of pillows. Her face lit up when she saw me. She looked relaxed and alert. Her eyes were clear. Had it not been for the video screens, the cylinders of oxygen, and the intravenous tubes surrounding her, one might imagine she had a mere case of flu. She pressed my hand and smiled gently, then asked for my husband. She and he were close. Nina kept stalking her grandmother, fluttering, making loud life sounds. "He's outside. They'll only allow two visitors at a time," I explained to my mother.

She turned to Nina. "Go, Ninele. I want to say hello to your father." Nina acquiesced, reluctantly, kissed her grandmother and told her, "I'll see you tomorrow." Before leaving, she adjusted two photographs of herself that she'd brought that morning and put within eyeshot of her grandmother. "Remember what I told you," said my mother, deliberately, emphatically, gazing at Nina intently. "Will you remember?" Nina nodded, kissed her again, and left. I wondered what confidence they'd exchanged. My husband entered.

Bella took his hand. "How are you, Danny?" Fine, he said. "Look at me," she went on. "Do you think I'll ever come out of this?" He reassured her.

They brought her dinner. Chicken, mashed potatoes, tea, Jell-O. She wanted only the tea. All day, fluids had been withheld in an effort to reduce her chest congestion. She was extremely dehydrated. Her lips were parched. She sipped the tea in small, eager sips. I offered her some food. She accepted a bit of mashed potatoes. The doctor, on his morning rounds, had told her that carbohydrates provided strength. So. She was still trying. I was encouraged. But she complained, "Don't feed me so fast." Oh, how I wanted to nourish her, inject her with vitality, stoke her with energy, like an anxious mother with a frail infant.

As I doled out the potatoes, a nurse entered. "I think you'd both better step outside." She glanced significantly at the cardiogram flashing alongside the bed. The yellow line on the graph was zigzagging irregularly, a human warning alert that the heart was skipping beats, though my mother showed no visible alteration or agitation.

From the corridor we saw the floor doctor enter. A brisk, matter-of-fact young woman in white, the stethoscope dangling on her starched lapels like a necklace. We waited. In about fifteen minutes she emerged, a roll of film bobbing from her hands, like a film editor. Before I could reach her, she had enclosed herself in the floor office. I knocked at the door. She scrutinized me with that glance of impatience and condescension reserved by staff for that superfluous, intrusive human element of family.

"How is she?" I asked.

"There's instability."

"Will she be all right?"

"She must rest. No one can go in to her now."

"Should we call her doctor?"

She was noncommittal.

My mother's personal physician was off-call for the weekend. An associate came in his stead and disappeared into the Intensive Care room. I spoke to him when he came out.

"It's a delicate balance," he told us. "We've put her on more dramatic intravenous medication." He was a kind man, Turkish perhaps, in his thirties, his sympathetic eyes so dark they seemed to be lined with kohl. I plied him with questions, floundering, not having the vocabulary within my grasp. He answered technically and directly. There was ultimately only one answer. It was a delicate balance.

I informed him that we'd ordered a private nurse, as on the previous night. Finally, he bid us go in and say good night.

The lamps in her room were out. The tubes invisible. The fine line on the cardiograph machine flickered steadily like a stream of fireflies on a still night. A dim light filtered in from the hall like a swathe of gauze. My mother was propped against her pillows, serene, looking very simple, girlish, comfortable, like a child in bed with a lingering cold and prepared for the night.

"How are you feeling, Mamele?" I asked.

She nodded sweetly. "I'm all right. Go home, children, get a good night's sleep. And don't worry."

My husband kissed her hands. I kissed her forehead. Those were her last words. *Don't worry.*

The next words I heard, awakened at 1:55 that morning, were from her doctor.

"We did all that we could."

Cardiac arrest. It's all over. To be cheated out of being with her at the last moment. Not to have had a last contact, a word, a glance. For her to tell me one more word, to tell me that ultimate intimate infinite message. For me to say one final word. To provide her with a last comfort. Oh, futile tenderness!

I awake in the middle of the night and tell myself, She's gone. My mother is dead. Never will I see her again. How to grasp this? How can it have happened to her? How can she have done it to me? I never truly believed she would ever die. Now she will not come if I call, even if I cry. The only way to find her is in sleep. Only in dreams can I see her alive, in everyday acts. Dispatching me to school, kneading dough, taking coffee cake from the oven, cleaning the chicken, hailing me from the window to toss down a coin wrapped in newspaper for the itinerant ice-cream vendor or the merry-go-round, airing the pillows and fluffing the pale-green goose-down quilt on the bed, sorting and pressing grapes for wine, amusing me when I was little with scary faces, pouring turpentine on my hair to delouse me, pinching my arm in anger, doling out in winter the morning dose of cod-liver oil, hemming my dress, accompanying me, at age sixteen, to the furrier for my first fur coat with matching muff bought from her household savings, rubbing my fevered chest with alcohol, applying a long sock filled with hot salt to my inflamed tooth, swimming in a cold New Hampshire lake, her head always above water, unwrapping the marketing—fresh heads of lettuce, a batch of sorrel, sturdy beet roots, leafy stalks of celery, strawberries, those first hard green peaches of summer. I see her putting drops in her eyes, rolling her silk stockings around elastic bands at her thigh, tilting a small felt hat over her eyes. In sleep she keeps coming to me. Younger than I am now. But in the daytime she's gone. My nurture is gone. My shelter. My protection. There's no tender, milk-fragrant flesh to envelop me in its underarm warmth. Only in dreams . . .

"Let me go," she told the doctors who were attempting to resuscitate her. So it was reported to me later by her night nurse. What did my mother think and see? Did she experience one of those fleeting reviews of childhood? Happy memories, from a time before her own mother's death? Did she see her house, the wooden house in Poland with its scrubbed floor? The cobbled stones of the village, the muddy back streets that became rutted with ice in winter? Was she holding her mother's hand as they went to market, carrying perhaps a basket between them, she one handle, her mother the other? Did she see the market jostling with people and horses, the squawk of crated fowl, the stands of fruits and vegetables? Or was she crossing the little wooden footbridge and going off into the woods to gather black

mushrooms with her friends? Barefoot she'd be, for
none of the children wore shoes in summer. Or was she
skinny-dipping in the icy pond by the woods? Maybe
she was sitting in the courtyard of her house playing
jacks with small flat uniform pebbles. Or was she seeing
the glow of her mother's face, head covered with a
shawl, as she blessed the Sabbath candles? Or her
father making a toast over a small glass of vodka? Was
she sitting in cheder with the other schoolchildren?
Wide-eyed boys with visored caps and earlocks, girls
with flowered kerchiefs on their heads? Was there a
parade of village characters who passed before her—
the knife grinder, the milkman, the scissors sharpener,
the umbrella maker, the tailor in vest, apron, and cap,
the chair mender, the water carrier, the horseradish
vendor, the street musician, the smithy, or the chimney
sweep? All those characters—Berele, Leib, Itzik,
Benya, Chaim, Mendel, Yankel, Peisya, Reisl, Yoyna,
Schmuhl—that she used to describe to me? The sexton
rapping on shutters to let people know that the Sabbath
was about to begin? The cat they put socks on at Pass-
over so he wouldn't bring in crumbs? Was she hearing
the chords of village mandolins that played for circle
dances? Did she hear faraway voices and tunes? What
did my mother see at the end? Her mother, her husband, her children? Was it all white like one of those
dreams of dazzling light? Whose was the last face she
saw? Not her child, not her grandchild.

Her corpse. The smooth forehead peering
from the white shroud. The temples, the forehead, the
sockets of the eyes more subtly molded than they had

been in life. No lines on the face. She looks younger. Due to the mortician's craft, or is it repose? Detachment? Her lips, frail as membranes, are barely closed, as if she might even breathe. Her cheek is cold under my lips.

An old saying: If you want to know about people, go to weddings and funerals. Many of those who attend my mother's funeral are the elderly tenants of her building, a typical West Side ten-story house on a side street off the Hudson. It is the building adjoining ours. Her neighbors come out on that snowy, slippery day, a day of blizzard, to say goodbye. An elder being mourned by her peers. She never complained, they say. We didn't even know she was sick. A blessing that she didn't suffer. She was a beautiful human being. Conventional phrases somehow restored to their original ring of truth. What are the thoughts of these elderly? Another friend gone. One more link with our generation gone. The chain gradually breaking. Mrs. Tolpen's appointment with death was closer than ours. We've more friends in the cemetery than out. My own friends come, too. I see their faces out of focus. They pass us, the mourners—my sister, myself, our husbands, six grandchildren: my three daughters, my sister's two daughters, and her son. Young people in their teens and early twenties huddled together in grief, old enough to understand the terminality of death. My sister's face is pale and blotched. The only face that registers clearly on me is my mother's. She lies in her coffin. I stand alongside her, wearing the navy silk-foulard dress that she bought for me on my last birthday.

The first name on the guest list at the chapel is Pee-Wee, a six-foot-three, handsome young black dude. He occupies an aisle seat in the last row. The same spot he always took when he came to our movie house, the New Yorker Theater, where Bella, the candy lady, would be positioned behind the glass showcase. From that post, for the fourteen years we ran the theater, she doled out paper cones of popcorn, Mounds bars, Mr. Goodbars, Chuckles and Chunkys, and Goldenberg's Peanut Chews. Pee-Wee loved my mother. He loved to talk to her, kid around with her. He dug her humor and savviness. She dug his street-smarts and wing-tipped shoes. On Christmas, he'd bring her a box of chocolates. On Valentine's Day, a plant. He called her Bella, like most everyone else.

The candy stand was a perfect perch for Bella. Film buffs grew to know the elderly woman who worked evenings. She had a special wise look one couldn't fail to recognize. An open gaze, unarmored by pretension or defensiveness. Friends of mine, unaware that she was my mother, mother-in-law of the theater owner, often struck up an independent friendship with her. She was the confidante of many. Women told her about child-rearing difficulties, impending divorces. Adolescents complained about impossible parents, confided their troubles. They could tell Bella things they wouldn't dream of telling their parents. It's always easier with someone of an alternate generation. Bella, moreover, was nonjudgmental. Though she might not approve of their acts, and told them so, she wouldn't reject them.

Old people, lonely widows, talked about their degenerative arthritis. José, the theater manager, a young, intelligent Cuban, kept her abreast of his burgeoning love affair with the cashier, a doctoral candidate in philosophy at City College. Bella listened, advised him, helped him decide between a striped or polka-dot tie, taught him Yiddish phrases. They cracked jokes. She invited him for potato latkes on Sunday morning. When certain customers, children or down-and-outers, fumbled for nonexistent change to pay for a candy bar, Bella would give a reduced rate, telling them they could pay some other time when they had the money.

She commiserated with those who didn't have extra coins for candy. After all, anyone who wanted candy should have it. Wasn't everyone a mother's child? Above all else, we must be kind to each other. There she sat atop her high stool, arranging the shelves, replenishing the empty spots, shining the counter glass till it squeaked and sparkled, filling the popcorn machine when she came in and emptying it when she left, whisking the last kernel away with a long-nosed brush, observing the stream of moviegoers who entered and departed, people finding laughter and tears on the big white screen inside with W. C. Fields, Charlie Chaplin, Buster Keaton, or Emil Jannings. In the daytime, she'd often go and catch the show, revivals especially. An old Preston Sturges movie, anything with Humphrey Bogart, Bette Davis, Clark Gable, or Paul Muni. An inveterate movie fan, she had a soft spot for the stars of the silent era—Rudolph Valentino, Clara Bow, Lillian Gish—and in fact identified the day of my birth as being the day *after* she saw *Dr. Jekyll and Mr. Hyde.*

Bella grew to know the New Yorker's regular customers, and they her, like a village pharmacist or postman. Even when they didn't buy candy, they stopped to say hello or to inquire about the film. Ozu's *Tokyo*

Story, what did she think of it? And Bresson's *Pick-pocket*? Did she, by the way, agree with Pauline Kael's rave review of *Breathless*, which had been blown up into a 40-by-60 display in front of the theater? Just wait, she tipped off a fan, till you see *Boudu Saved from Drowning*. Such a moving story.

Poor Pee-Wee. He sits in the end seat of the last row in the chapel, listening to the rabbi read from Proverbs —"Her children rise up, and call her blessed"—listening to the cantor chant a final song for Bella. Pee-Wee rises with all of us for the Hebrew prayer and drops his head to say Amen.

Grief comes in unexpected surges. As when nursing, and anything can trigger the onrush of milk. An infant in a carriage or a child crying, but also a traffic light changing, water running, a dog barking. Grief comes out of cups and saucers, empty platforms, hooting whistles, a foghorn blowing, sparrows chirping, sirens screeching, a piano playing, a fern unfurling on my window, tender white mushrooms leaning against one another in their box. Little alarms these are, transmitted to that network of nerves, muscle, hormone, tissue, and cells that constitute the physical self. Mysterious cues that set off a reminder of grief. It comes crashing like a wave, sweeping me in its crest, twisting me inside out. Then recedes, leaving me broken. Oh, Mama, I don't want to eat, to walk, to get out of bed. Reading, working, cooking, listening, mothering. Nothing matters. I do not want to be distracted from my grief. I wouldn't mind dying. I wouldn't mind it at all. I wake from sleep in the middle of every night and say to myself, "My mother is dead!"

I wake up. The body refreshed and betrayed by sleep. But then I remember. A new day. New and old. The light filters through the blinds, the scabs open and bare the raw hidden places. It is too early in the day for tears. The morning numbness is a dull, constant pain. Time, previously precious and pressing, crammed with busywork, projects, and intentions, flaps now on its tall mast. Only routine tasks catch me in their doltish hold and propel me through a let's pretend of living. I'm a sleepwalker prodded by the commands of a dream. To obey the dictates of a person I've ceased to be.

Make the bed, stray into the kitchen, feed the birds, water the plants, put up coffee, empty the dishwasher, take in the newspapers, acknowledge my family, butter toast, fulfill a role. Things happen one after the other. Coffee boils over, a teaspoon drops, the telephone rings, the Con Edison man comes to read the meter.

Breakfast over, and everyone gone, I trail through a house suddenly too large, too hollow, and too cluttered. There is no place I care to sit. No place I want to stand. Everywhere I land, I am restless, misplaced. Bewildered. Strained. Deeply idle and empty. Yet, at the same time, expectant, as if this were some special sort of day. The air in the living room is charged with the perfume of lilies. Where can my friends have found lilies in February? The tall ivory chalices reel in their vases. I stroke the petals of the pale blossoms. My fingers come away stippled with golden dust.

The silent room is charged with an invisible agitation. A day begins. A whole day to be lived through. To be died through. I feel depleted at the onset. Physical exhaustion, mental lassitude. The difference between

sleep and waking has diminished; wakefulness is merely
more painful. I stand in front of the window. Hating the
flamboyant coleus plant that flaunts its lewd greens and
purples on the windowsill, the rank and rowdy snake
plant that thrusts forth invulnerable stalks. Outside,
black trunks, black sun, black telephone poles, zero
weather. New York digging out from a blizzard. A cold
wind shuddering over Riverside Drive. Barges and tug-
boats coming and going on the ice-crested Hudson
River, cars rolling to destinations over the gray band of
the West Side Highway, on side streets and on the distant glittering hump of the George Washington Bridge.
New Jersey smokestacks, inches away.

In the frost-flowered pane, I see my mother's face.
Ten days now since she died. Across the street, a
woman at the window is brushing her hair. Ten days . . .
Above, a leaden, uncaring sky peers down at little toy
people scurrying toward intersections. Ten days . . .

A car bleats below. *The New York Times* straddles
the living-room chair. Headlines: CITY PARALYZED BY
BLIZZARD. WAR IN ANGOLA. SOVIET DISSIDENTS FACE
TRIAL. The words glide past me like unmarked cars.

The day after her death, my doorbell rings,
and in the hallway beneath a stiff, gray felt hat stands
Mr. Weinberg, the tall, dignified patriarch who lives
on my mother's floor. An observant Jewish elder, he
doesn't shake my hand, say hello or how are you. It is
not the orthodox custom after death. His greeting, in
Yiddish, bids me long life. Mr. Weinberg enters my life
unbidden, taking it upon himself to structure death and
mourning in accordance with Jewish tradition.

He reminds me, in deference to the dead, to arrange the funeral as soon as possible, to cover the mirrors in the house, to light the symbolic funerary lamp of remembrance, to provide a simple casket, to wear an old garment continuously for the seven days of sitting shivah (*shivah* being the Hebrew word for seven).

I nod, recalling the seven days when my father long ago sat for his parents on a low mourning stool, unshaven, wearing carpet slippers, sometimes only socks. I remember those collections of relatives who sat with him, his sisters, some now dispersed, others dead, the women without makeup, all sitting, exchanging memories of the deceased and receiving visitors. We ate hard-boiled eggs. I remember the prayers of the men who gathered at the house.

Mr. Weinberg takes charge. He arranges for a minyan, ten men over the age of thirteen, to attend the chapel service, and also contacts a rabbi, an American educated by the Hasidim in Brooklyn yeshivas and at Union Theological Seminary. The rabbi, who'd been acquainted with my mother, would deliver the eulogy. Mr. Weinberg has also invited a revered cantor to the chapel, a man noted for his chants at services for the virtuous. "Your mother was a fine woman—*eine feine frau*," says Mr. Weinberg. He offers to say Kaddish for her twice daily at his synagogue for a year, until the gravestone is erected and unveiled.

Throughout my first week of disorientation and grief, the aged patriarch visits me daily. I accept these visitations, startled at first by their unannounced nature, but soon yielding to and welcoming them. Always they begin with that ritualistic *Zul lang leben*, "I wish you long life," an utterance I can recall my father having used through the years during occasional lapses into Yiddish—affectionate moments of greeting or of play when he reverted to the language of the breast. It was also the traditional blessing when we sneezed.

During those seven days of prescribed mourning, this pious man, whom I barely know, merely in the way one knows, nods, and greets people on one's block, this elderly Jew who speaks little English, and whom I answer in my primitive Yiddish, provides a measure of consolation. Often we simply sit in silence. Other times, he will try to shepherd me gently into the fold of practicing Judaism. Each time I see him to the door, he gazes wistfully at the spot alongside the jamb where observant Jews hang a mezuzah, that small white capsule which consecrates the home and contains a miniature parchment with printed verses from Deuteronomy. "Would it hurt to hang one?" he asks. I shake my head. No, it wouldn't hurt. Never have I the heart to flatly refuse him, yet I know that in the end I won't conform. It isn't my way. We exchange glances. I, a first-generation American, non-observant, pragmatic; he, a refugee of the war, a bearer and transmitter of the Scroll and of the acts of faith and conformity that lead to God and salvation.

Visiting the bereaved is a mitzvah, a good deed which the Torah enjoins upon its followers. As the rabbi remarked on our return drive from the cemetery: "It took five generations to produce a Bella." He was referring to her way of being in the world, her Yiddishkeit, or Jewishness, her spirit. Likewise, it took five generations to create a Mr. Weinberg, this traditional observant Jew who accepts death yet exhorts the survivor: *Zul lang leben.*

KADDISH

Blessed and praised, glorified and exalted, extolled and honored, adored and lauded be the name of the Holy One, blessed be He, beyond all blessings and hymns, praises and consolations that are ever spoken in the world.

Yisgadal v'yiskadash sh'meh rabbo, b'olmo deevro chiruseh, v'yamlich malchuseh, b'chayechon uvyomechon, uv'chayey d'chol beys yisroel, ba-agolo uvizman koreev v'imru omen.

Y'he sh'meh rabbo m'vorach l'olam ulolmey olmayo.

Yisborach v'yishtabach v'yispo-ar v'yisromam v'yisnaseh v'yis-hador v'yisaleh v'yis-hallol sh'meh d'kud'sho b'reech hu, l'elo (ul'elo) min col birchoso v'shiroso tushb'choso v'nechomoso, daamiron b'olmo, v'imru omen.

Y'he sh'lomo rabbo min sh'mayo v'chayim olenu v'al col yisroel, v'imru omen.

Oseh sholom bimromov hu ya-aseh sholom olenu v'al col yisroel, v'imru omen.

She lived in the house next door. A week after her death I go there. The nameplate along the row of bells for apartment 7D is marked JOSEPH TOLPEN. Their letter box, too. Though my father had been dead seven years, my mother had not removed his name. Her apartment is just as she left it, as if she'd stepped out for an errand or a stroll, meaning to return. A glass with some coffee saved from the morning brew stands on the cupboard, covered with an inverted saucer. In the sink is a small, white enamel saucepan which she intended to wash on her return. I rinse the pot and set it on the drainboard.

Some bananas in a little basket on the sill have ripened. The plants need watering. The soil sucks up the water in thirsty gulps. I place the bananas in the refrigerator. Inside are the oranges from the last batch I brought so that during the blizzard she herself would not attempt to carry a heavy load.

I sit within her walls and cry. Her smell is all around. Her house robe drapes the living-room chair, as if she hadn't had the time or strength on that last day before going to the doctor to put it away. Her blue scuffs are by her bed, parallel to each other, the cotton quilt coverlet with its yellow trellis vines is punctuated by the red heart of the old-fashioned hot-water bottle left upon it. Did she have the chills that morning, or had she used it the night before?

Oh, my dear mother! How can I accept that you are gone? Your presence fills these rooms, every object in it is a memory trace of my childhood. How can I believe that *that* part is over?

The next day I come again. This time, I ring the bell of apartment 7E, the one facing hers. Mr. Weinberg's. He has requested, and I have promised, some of my mother's furnishings, including her TV. His small, frail wife, who also speaks little English and seldom leaves their apartment, returns with him and me; she carries out the curtains, the rods, the shades, some lamps. He removes the rocker, the matching leather-tooled lamp tables, the kitchen chairs, and then tries to wedge the bulky kitchen table out the narrow kitchen door. Amazing, this old man, the very man who provided spiritual consolation during my period of shivah, this man who carries a pacemaker inside his chest, has the impulse, the energy, the hopefulness to acquire new objects. Doesn't he realize it? My mother has died. His turn is soon—who knows, maybe next.

This is a man who witnessed the Holocaust, who was forced several times to abandon an old life and cherished objects to start anew. Ousted from his home in Rumania, he fled to Lithuania, then to Tashkent, where he and his small family were stranded for three years. An uprooted Eastern European Jew transplanted to the torrid heat of one of central Asia's oldest cities, the capital of Uzbek.

Yet somehow Mr. Weinberg persists as if his time on earth is forever, though as a man of religion his view is of eternity. Mr. Weinberg persists, as patient as a spider whose web is continuously brushed off the ceiling with a broom. Like newlyweds, he and his wife scurry about, gathering objects from my mother's world to reassemble in their own rooms. The pitiful energy of humans! They bring to mind my pet lovebirds, to whom I once presented a nest which I'd brought from the country, hoping to wheedle them into laying eggs, producing offspring. The female promptly undid that rustic nest, used the materials to make her own, laid a beautiful egg. Her mate consumed the egg on the second day. Clever bird. Instinctive birth control.

Ah, huffing and puffing Mr. Weinberg. Foolhardy man! Deluded, absurd, relentless man. Alive man! Mutely, I watch him lifting, straining, calculating door widths, table angles. Dimensions. At last, I give him a hand and shove him and his wife out the door.

My mother's apartment is not hard to empty. She left us no complicated task. A simple woman, unacquisitive, not a hoarder, she never required that security of hanging on to possessions. What she didn't use, she gave away over the years. A Persian-lamb jacket to my sister, a beaded bag to my daughter, a silk kimono to my niece. Discarded sweaters and blouses found their way to my cleaning woman.

In the closet, I find her good dresses hung inside out to protect them from fading. The blue silk taffeta worn at my wedding, the polka-dot chiffon at my nephew's bar mitzvah, the soft challis chemises that she wore every day. In a bureau drawer, I find old photographs from Europe and my father's phylacteries, two little black leather boxes, one to be placed on the left arm during morning prayer, the side closest to the heart, the other on the head, close to the brain. I find his white silk shawl with its blue stripes, his yarmulke, the silk skullcap, his prayer books, a book of lectures by Eugene Debs, an elementary English grammar. A brief, abridged history of an immigrant's early sojourn in America.

In the kitchen I face my mother's china with the blue scrollwork pattern familiar to me from childhood. I find the white enamel saltbox for kosher salt, and a pale-blue teapot containing a curl from my first haircut.

In the hall closet hang her coats. The good spring coat, like her dresses, hangs inside out. On the top shelf is an oversized roaster for Thanksgiving turkeys; pots grow smaller as one's family diminishes. Alongside, I find a stack of my father's ancient bookkeeping ledgers, ordinary black-and-white notebooks, the sort schoolchildren use. Why did she save those? I find my old diary, a chronicle of my tenth year. And my sister's wedding gown. The hall closet, depository of a family's archives.

From the wall I remove the photographs. Her daughters' wedding pictures, grandchildren at various ages, a faded photograph of myself at age one covered with a plaid baby shawl, another at around twelve, rigged up in a tap-dancing costume à la Eleanor Powell—top hat, cane, the works. I can still remember my mortification that summer of my twelfth year when I was performing an acrobatic solo at the annual show and the strapless top of my two-piece costume snapped and fell off on stage. The audience laughed at the contretemps. I burst into tears and fled from the stage. I could imagine all those weasel-eyed twelve-year-old boys razzing me for life. My mother urged me to go back on. I didn't. Instead, I got mad at her for saying, "It's not the end of the world. What have you got to show?" True, I was flat-chested. But that was the point.

On the shelf by the door stands a large gallon wine jug. It is filled with berries and vodka.

"Would you like a taste?" I can hear her say, her tone lighthearted and tempting. "The flavor improves every day!" The plump red strawberries and blueberries floating in their liquor bath blur before my eyes.

I stand in the empty vestibule, remembering how she'd see me to the door, how I'd glance over my shoulder from the hall at that gentle face with its soft melting smile and watch her go into the house by herself.

Her handbag. They call from the hospital to come for her handbag and "personal effects." On that

last ambulatory day, that Tuesday, she was carrying
the tan calfskin handbag with a double strap that I'd
brought her from Verona three years ago. She loved the
handbag because it was lightweight and soft as glove
leather. At first, she permitted herself the luxury of
using it only on special occasions. After that first year of
initiation, it became her everyday handbag, *the* handbag.
Now my husband goes and gets it from the hospital, discreetly places it in his study closet, along with a shopping
bag containing her clothes, and a small pillow bought by
my niece for her to rest her arm on, the arm pierced with
the intravenous tube. Her blue winter coat also gets
hung in my husband's closet. A coat she and I shopped
for two winters ago at B. Altman's.

I take the handbag from the closet. It contains what
it has always contained. Keys, some tissues, a change
purse filled with too many pennies and too much
change, some hard coffee candies, two packages of
chewing gum, though she never chewed. The gum was
for my daughters, who always considered Bella's purse
as mutual property. They rummaged at will for the Life
Savers and coffee candies and gum which they knew
they'd find. There is no comb or compact, items my
mother didn't carry. I also find an unredeemed pink
laundry slip.

I lay the candies on my desk. Her final offering. The
tissues, ordinary dispensable slips of paper, transparent
layers of bark, I place inside my top drawer.

Why didn't the doctors warn me from the
start? Those damn medicine men who know so much,
with their machines, and their handshakes, and their
routine procedures, and their tranquilized linoleum

glances and their cheerful "You be a good girl now" and their fat fees, and custom-cut suits and vests. Why didn't they tell me: Now. Give her all that she wants. All the love, all the nourishment, all the thank you's. Soon it will be too late. Exchange that comprehensive gaze which a departing traveler casts upon a person or landscape to bear away in memory the face or view to which he may never return. Even Don Juan was fore-warned by the messenger of death: *Ya es tarde*. Now it is too late!

Her lips were so dry! The nurses allowed her no water. If it was the end, what starched medical princi-ple were they trying to prove? Why couldn't I have given her everything to please her? Cold ginger ale, tea, soothing vanilla ice cream? The last alms granted before death. Why couldn't they have told me? So that I could have been there, holding her hand, warming her cooling flesh with the heat of my life, letting her cling to me, feeling our bond as she groped her way through that final darkness. One hour before death you are still alive. Why couldn't I have led her gently to the starting place of that dark solitude so that as she wandered into the final separation, as the world receded, growing dimmer and further and then fading altogether, she'd hear my voice, my words, my echo, even fading away, telling her that it was all right? Why couldn't they have said: *Now! Now's the time. Stay!*

I walk the street, along Amsterdam Avenue, where I am not known, where I will go unrecognized. Everything is black and white. Without color. The street lined with shops that sell bread, fish, pots, mortars and pestles, thimbles, thumbtacks, shoes,

gloves, linoleum, TV sets, emery boards, all the useful
things she no longer needs. That I do not want.
Bodegas garlanded in necklaces of garlic and sausages.
Mangoes, yucas, plantains tumbling in cheerful heaps.
The window of the *botánica* teeming with wooden
santos, incense lamps, herbal teas, and amulets. What
magic can bring her back? Post offices, schools,
churches, banks, libraries, all seem strange, the sunshine unreal and artificial. Streams of people walk
toward me, away from me. Maybe, maybe among all
those faces I will find her. Bump into her. She'll be
carrying some small package. Her face will light up at
the pleasure of running into me. Maybe if I walk and
walk I will find her. If I walk to the very end of the
street, to the tip of the island. My feet consume the
streets, mechanically, as if carried on an escalator.
Faces pass. Hers is not among them. I walk alone. No
one is behind me. Protecting me. Encouraging me. I
cry. Not the stifled sob in an elevator jammed with
people or perhaps only one curious onlooker, or in a
darkened movie house, or in bed even, before my husband falls asleep, but openly, fully. I cry with the total-
ness of a hurt child. Of a child desperately clinging to a
mother's hand amid a chaotic mob. Clutching mistakenly
at a person deemed from the ground to be the mother,
only to discover that it is merely a dim, bleary-eyed view
of her. The little sweaty hand is gripping air. Fingers
dangle empty. She's been snatched away. You are
stranded. There is no lost-and-found depot for waifs
where mother will come and find her darling. How I
yearn for her. Ache for her. No one can soothe me. She's
not here to say: *Don't cry.* To kiss away my injury.
Never again will she console me or praise me or hear me
out or laugh at some funny episode. I want to place my

head in her lap, or take her in my arms and touch her hair. I want *her*. Not her spirit. I search for her face in the streets, but find it nowhere.

My back aches. A dormant condition, dating from whiplash suffered in an automobile accident fifteen years ago, resurfaces. The spine protests supporting me upright. A burning jab shoots into my right Achilles' heel at each flexion of the arch. My feet are loath to propel me. A corkscrew twinge darts through my left collarbone every time my head turns. My belly feels raw as in menstrual cramps, and flabby as if I'd just given birth. Usually tight and muscular, the belly seems to be drawing away from its center, from the spinal column, as if in escape. My whole body balks, limping through a world in which she is absent. Grief floods the bloodstream, permeates the bowels, the marrow. My body, torn from its mooring, speaks in a language of its own.

Shortly after her death, I go to have my hair cut and crimped. I, who've always worn it long and straight, or severely drawn into a bun, stare into the hairdresser's mirror at a woman with hair frizzing around her face. A throwback to those Shirley Temple curls of mine which, at age five, I insisted upon shearing, pestering my mother to accompany me to the beauty parlor for my first haircut. She sat quietly, her hands folded, watching the scissors snip off the curls, seeing them roll down the sheet around my neck to fall in a circle on the floor. Afterward, while I was still mounted on the wooden, painted pony that had been set on the seat to raise me to hairdresser level, she looked at my bobbed hair and newly bared neck. She smiled and said, "You look nice." Then she stooped and picked up one curl to save.

In the morning when I see myself in the mirror I'm astonished at the bizarre stranger reflected there. I avert my eyes and stand in front of the window to brush my teeth. Tenants in our building, colleagues at the university, merchants, friends who've known me always with long hair remark on the change. "You look so different." "It's flattering." "It makes you look younger." Is that what I want? For people to recognize me as different from before? To know that I'm not the same— that I'll never be the same?

From my drawer I take a thin black wedding band and place it on my finger alongside my plain gold one. A badge of mourning.

So this is what they mean by growing up. Peekaboo, hide-and-seek, little games to get you ready for the real thing. The canny child is properly anxious. He knows, the way kids know, that it is not all raisins and almonds, as the lullaby promises. We cajole him through the years into believing that he won't be abandoned. But all along he suspects the hoax. Children's lore attests to it. *Don't swing your legs, else Mama will die. Step on a crack, break Mama's back.* The four-year-old whimpers when deposited that first day in nursery school. When he comes home, she may be gone. The first thing he calls out on opening the front door is: "Mommy?" And when the reassuring "Yes" or "I'm here" comes from an unseen voice at the other end of the house, he can drop his books and freely go out to play. He's confirmed her existence. But she does go away. At which point begins the real growing up. Maturing, they call it. You're no longer Mama's child, her little darling, her golden one, the apple of her eye for whom she saves the heel of the bread, or the chicken liver. Her eyes are permanently shut, pressed down in the dark by metal disks. All is provisional, the dream of eternity is a child's bedtime story calculated to soothe. The lost tooth, the outgrown clothes, ashes, ashes all fall down. Your mama was an offering, not on permanent loan.

Why, silly, you knew it all along. Every time you took a trip, with every long goodbye, that was the fear. The dread. In almost everything you wrote, the theme was separation. As the Spaniards say, *Cada loco tiene su manía*, Every madman has his theme.

Grow up. Put away your paper dolls. You're no more a knee baby. You have your husband, your daughters, your friends, your work, your own life to lead. The dependence on her was undoubtedly excessive, the way you're carrying on. You knew all along that people die. Your father died, hordes of people die in wars, accidents, extermination camps, of hunger. It's a commonplace. Happens all the time.

Remember that late-December afternoon some twenty years ago? You were pushing a stroller with your daughter inside, it was on West Ninety-first Street, and though early evening, already dark, and the streets icy and slippery. The child's nose was runny and her breath blew frosty puffs into the cold night as she babbled some run-on chant, when suddenly an elderly man in homburg hat and cane stumbled in front of you. Thinking he'd tripped on the ice, you put the brake on the stroller and moved to help him to his feet. You raised his head into the crook of your arm. His face was chalky under the street lamp. His eyes urgent. Suddenly he gave a wisp of a gasp and died in your arms. It often happens that way. The banality of death.

All of us, we're merely renting space in life. Statutory tenants. Resign yourself to mortality. To your humanness. As sure as the sea is swayed by the moon, so do our lives wind up on the shore of memory. You, too, are not invulnerable. As your mother walked out on you, so will your turn come. You have your life, so claim it. And your death. Claim that, too.

Was it Voltaire who remarked that the human race is the only one that knows it must die? And Unamuno, who centuries later reiterated that the flight from death is what distinguishes man from animals. Indeed, you're next in line. Number one. Número uno. Maybe that's what's bothering you. In this mourning are you not perhaps mourning for yourself as well as your mother? She has given you the cue. Her last lesson. Life is a loan and the payment is death. So, what's new? Remember those teenage swoonings over Omar Khayyam's Rubaiyat? Ah, the transience of life. Of course, I've known life's conditions all along. But. Go and accept them.

Now there's no more conceiving myself to be on that upward slope of the parabola. Deceiving myself. The sled is on its downward curve and there's no way to dodge the fatal goalpost. The dead end. No way. In fact, the speed picks up toward the bottom. Aging. The days go fast, my mother used to say. So steer carefully.

Ahead lie fresh sorrows, and scattered felicity. What does it all mean? An infinitesimal instant since that day three billion years ago when this fiery mass of our planet was hurtled from the sun. Still, our solar apron strings remain unbroken. While spinning on our axis we continue to revolve around the sun. Spinning and spinning, despite the knowledge that there's an end to individual existence. That's life. It's nature's way to be ousted from the snug cocoon of the round motherless earth upon whose curve all must one day sink.

Mourning in many ways is like falling in love. An isolation, an impoverishment, a shrinking, a contraction of concerns and interests. All-consuming, blinding, it absents you from the world and absorbs you totally. It represses all other feelings and life contents. You seem to be filled with it. Always. In a sense, like pregnancy. But unlike the quickening of pregnancy, here a lead weight lodges in your stomach. Whereas pregnancy imparts a sense of doing something even while inactive, mourning bequeaths a sense of futility and meaninglessness in the midst of activity. It creates disorder in your network of mental habits. I write on the blackboard, read a book, screen a film, pare carrots, speak on the telephone. Phantom gestures, flickers on an empty screen. Her death is the only thing on my mind. It commands my attention. When I get up, go to sleep, when I dress, and bathe, cook and eat, or awaken in the middle of the night. It shares with falling in love total surrender and withdrawal. It is the only thing that counts.

There are tribes that bury in fetal position. The dead are laid into the earth as once they lay in the womb. The woman's oh! of childbirth trails into the ah! of death. And, in between, briefly, life's steady tickings. The throb of pulse, the in-and-out of breath, sighs, whispers, dialogues, endearments, plaints, a steady whir of life sounds, like birds thrumming the air. And then silence. The voyage of life drops anchor. You live only to die, my mother used to say. Knees drawn up, I lie in fetal position. The house is still. Behind shut eyes flash eidetic images, scenes from the past, yet strain as I will I'm unable in that deep silence to hear her voice. That is the hardest to recall. My mother was once my vessel. I shared the throb of her body, vibrated to the pulse of her placenta, our vessels interchanged blood, fluids, nourishment, life. I rocked in that cradle of amniotic suspension. Shared that original unity. Now in fetal position, I am curled into myself.

Reduced, depleted, empty. I've no smile, no reflection, no shadow, no echo. I am stripped without her. Gone is that old sense of abundance, of surplus. Making, doing, anticipating, planning. Gone the desire to bake cake, preserve fruit, file clippings, press flowers, root plants, the impulse to hold, conserve, store. Camphoring clothes. For what? Let the moths get them. Why save empty jars for refilling, old notebooks for jottings, twists of string for future gifts, rubber bands? Vegetable juices for hearty stocks, a handful of almonds for a sauce, the heel of the bread for crumbs, a bit of Roquefort for salad dressing, the crust of cake for pudding? Not everything has a comeback. Not everything can be recycled. Formerly, I hadn't the heart to throw away a scrap of food, a remnant of fabric, old shoes, archaic hats, outmoded skirts. There seemed always a way of reintegrating odds and ends into the comings and goings of life. The cycle of fashion, after all, is like the rotation of crops. One season a field is turned to potatoes, the next oats. One season long skirts, the next short. Those purple suede shoes with T-strap and Cuban heel will eventually stage a comeback. Padded shoulders, passé one year, "in" the next. Beaded bags, kimono dresses—wait long enough and all the castoffs enjoy a second chance, a revival, a reincarnation. But now nothing seems worth saving. The rainy day has come, my savings are useless. Inconvertible currency. My mother epitomized my past, my present, my future. She encouraged me to save, to hope. To replenish old goose-down feathers with new, to sew fresh tickings, to wash grapes and ferment them in casks not too tightly sealed, to sort June strawberries and preserve them in vodka for February toddies. She sent me to the bank at age ten to open my first Christmas Club account, little weekly fifty-cent deposits which accrued into end-of-year bonanzas. As she said, you need bread to make a sandwich. But now my motion of preservation toward the future has died with her.

How does one grow accustomed to the void? Recover from the impact of the blow? Learn to live with rawness? To breathe deep though the umbilicus has ceased to breathe? Our cord is severed. I am upside down in a strange, incomprehensible place. How not to communicate my fear?

The therapy of water. Soaking in a hot tub, opening the faucet a crack to admit a steady trickle of water. Steam rises all around. Water laps at my chin. I can cry unheard.

Sleep, a sanctuary. In dreams I go back to places once so dear to me. Recapturing corridors and corners of my childhood. Sometimes I can't go in. Sadness seizes me, for I know that if I push too hard I will awake. And I do. I wait impatiently for the dream, for the fugitive landscape and figure to come back, to become a child again, to feel happy because everything is still possible and the inner monologue intact.

A dream: My mother has prepared a wicker basket brimming with fruit and vegetables: lettuce, cabbage, artichokes, peaches, pomegranates, grapes. I accompany her then to a certain liquor store which stocks her favorite apricot brandy. With a pleased look, she tucks the bottle into a corner of the basket.

My mother walks in my dreams.

I had one plan. She another. On January 16, when I dropped in at her apartment, it was cold outside and gray. One of those midwinter spells which turn New York into a muted, arctic city, granted only brief northern lights. A city bereft of rays or shadows. Sooty ruffles of old snow bordered the streets as on a dirty neck. The sidewalks were slippery, and pedestrians stumbled from one destination to another, gazing only at their feet, never lingering. It was around five in the afternoon.

She came to the door in her yellow quilted wrapper. Her face lit up on seeing me. We sat in the kitchen and she offered me a bowl of soup. I asked about her day. Well, she'd dressed and set out for a walk, but turned back because of the wind and icy streets. What's the use of going out on a day like this, she said. I had to agree. One couldn't stroll or sit on a park bench. Anyhow, I thought, no point looking for trouble at age seventy-four, particularly when recovering from a cold as she was. Silently, I regretted her day's isolation and recalled a remark she once made: "When I go outside, the bad goes out and the good comes in."

We talked around familiar topics. She commented on a new blouse that I was wearing, said that I looked good in the color red. And then she asked the true question on her mind: Are you really going to Seville? I rolled my eyes and pulled a face on her. She returned it with unflinching innocence. I couldn't believe the woman's persistence. Was I really going? I was counting the days. Andalusian sunshine, the sounds of Castilian, Moorish streets and gardens, olives and sherry. I had a hunger to be in Spain, having been away for almost ten years. Why must this mother of mine always resist our trips? Report to us every air crash broadcast on the radio as if she were hired by the railroads and ocean liners to compile the ultimately damning study on plane disasters? She'd never reconciled herself to airplane travel. Each of our trips was a wrench. Before going abroad, we'd eased our way into announcing it to her. How do you explain to someone who has no yen to travel why you want to leave your comfortable home with its clean linen, pure water, and pasteurized milk for the rigors of Yucatán, Marseilles, or Agrigento? The hinterlands. Did other daughters phone their mothers each time they descended a plane in one piece? I sighed, cocked my head, and eyed her chidingly. "Mom, how can you be such a back number? Of course we're going, you know we're going. We have our tickets, our hotel reservations, all arrangements have been made." I waited for her snappy rejoinder. When are you going? she asked. She knew full well, at least I think she knew, but I went along with the ritual. On February 9, I told her, during intersession. She nodded and murmured in Yiddish: *Geh mir gesinterheyt*—Go in good health.

I waited for another remark, a provocation. Nothing came. Putting on a cheerful tone, I switched the subject to the purpose of my visit, which was to invite her for dinner. But she said no, she'd just gotten out of her clothes and didn't feel like dressing again. She felt comfortable, she said. Lately, more and more she'd been begging off coming for dinner, joining us at a movie, taking a drive with my sister and her family. In retrospect, it seems as if she were zeroing in on home base, withdrawing from the external world to her own. Was this a deliberate preparation, a farewell, this turning inward, this reduction of her sphere of activity? I tried to persuade her, nagged even. I was preparing a favorite dish of hers, I wanted to show her a new watercolor that Nina had painted. "Please." She raised her hand to cut short my harangue. If I persisted, she'd be calling me a pest in another minute.

Her days went fast, she remarked. I hadn't asked. But I knew, sort of, how her days went. Simple. Breakfast, music and news on the radio, tidying the house, rinsing some small garments by hand, a bath, a walk, a bit of marketing, a telephone conversation with an old friend or distant relative, an early dinner, possibly a drop-in visit from a daughter, a grandchild or son-in-law. A shared cup of tea and undisjointed time for talking with them.

I often thought about my mother's day and how she filled time now that she wasn't working at the theater. Time never seemed a pressure to her. Though largely alone, she didn't complain about boredom or loneliness. That afternoon she did complain about her medications, an anticoagulant, potassium tablets, pills for glaucoma. She abhorred medicine. "I don't feel myself when I take them! One day I'll throw them all out," she said challengingly, and rose from the table to rinse the coffee cups. As she emptied the dregs and turned the faucet on hard, I had the feeling she was dumping her entire medicine chest. She also went on to complain about a neighbor who had dropped in on her that day and lingered for hours, boasting about her children, their sumptuous parties, their pearl-gray Mercedes-Benz, their Teaneck estate. "When I'm not feeling well, I like to be alone," my mother said. It was the first concrete mention of not feeling well.

I chatted about other topics, nothing abrasive. Those days I tried to tell her only good things. Things that would not upset her. After all, there comes a time in your eighth decade when you deserve to hear good things. To be assured that life is going well for your offspring, that your life was worthwhile. Today her attention seemed diminished. She was, in a way, detached. Then, on her own, she raised a problem my oldest daughter was having, and concluded reflectively, "Her problems are healthy problems." She paused, and added, "Sometimes I wish I'd just drop dead. I can't cope with it!"

We stared at each other for a long bleak moment, listening to the radiator cricking the steam. I broke the silence: "Please come and have dinner with us tonight, Mama." She shook her head.

That was the day of omens, presentiments, signals. That was the day she struck a new note. When she gave the secret away. Why did I not pick up the cue? Why did I not sense that diminution of strength? That ultimate seclusion? Could I not foresee that it might be

only months, weeks, days, hours before she'd be lost?
That I had to seize our remaining time and share it if
time is indeed possible to share? Was I too eager for my
own plan to recognize that she had another? She, too,
was going somewhere. Why didn't death give me a
clearer sign?

She saw me to the door, and in the vestibule asked,
"Would you like a taste of brandy?" We both glanced
toward the shelf at the gallon jug.

I told her no and kissed her. Her forehead was moist,
slightly perspiring.

She stood in the threshold as I waited in the hall for
the elevator. The indicator flashed the progress of its
ascent. We waited in silence. She knew exactly what
was going on in my mind: she knew that I was dream-
ing of Seville. When the elevator came, I repeated my
question: "Are you *sure* you won't come for dinner? I'll
wait for you to dress." God, how persistent and boring I
was!

She shook her head and smiled faintly.

"Have a good night."

As the elevator door closed, I saw her turn and go
into her apartment. No matter how many times I
watched her do this, it always produced a wrench in
me. Is this not, after all, one of our deepest fears? Old
and alone. *Alayn*, that Yiddish word of awesome
resonance. Alone.

The ancients had a favored question: Where
is the seat of the soul? The heart, the head, the spleen,
the liver, the belly? For the Greeks, the midriff con-
stituted the seat of consciousness. For the Indians and
Hebrews, the heart. For me it is the belly. The belly

that fills with life, warms with pleasure, and aches with emptiness. The penetrating jab of abortion, of hysterectomy. An empty chamber of raw endings, blood-engorged organs, quivering tissue, dangling nerve fibers, cords connected to nothing. A severed uterus. I feel my mother's absence deep in my belly. As if she'd been ripped from the core of my own flesh.

It's as if I've lost a child. Lately, I was her mother. Deceptive in age, she appeared younger than she was. She had a terrific pair of legs which she was proud of, and her stride was light, like that of a young woman. When she shook hands her grip was strong, and when she spoke her voice was firm and expressive. She liked to kid around with young people, to pass the time with them. She didn't care to be addressed deferentially or fussed over, didn't cultivate veneration. One never thought of Bella as old.

When my father died and she lived alone, I was concerned about her. A heart attack during the night, a fall, burglars. But at no point would she consider moving in with us; she valued her privacy and independence. Each day I'd call to check on her. Did you sleep well, have you had your coffee, did you take your digitalis? If it was a nasty day, I'd ask: "Do you need anything? Fresh milk, oranges?" It didn't matter what I said, or what she said, I was listening for the tone of her voice, the gauge of her well-being. One morning she laughingly remarked: "Did you call to see if I'm alive?" Plainspoken, ironic, canny.

My mother in the last years became part of my field of mothering. I thought of ways to please her. In country dry-goods stores I found cotton-flannel nightgowns, the kind they used to make, without synthetics. On birthdays, I bought her soft sweaters and sheer lacy scarves—garments that were not itchy. When I planted cucumbers, I seeded Kirbys to put up those garlic dill pickles she was so fond of. When I made soup, I cooked a double pot to bring her some. I baked cheesecake, her favorite. When she came to dinner, I'd urge her, like a coaxing mother, to eat, served her the parts she preferred—the wing of the turkey, the outer, crispy cut of beef, the crusty part of the cake. My freezer still holds a batch of cheese manicotti destined for our next meal together. I knew how much sugar went into her coffee, and how much cream. I served the soup too hot, the way she liked it. I knew her tastes, her habits, the physical way in which she occupied the world. I wanted to nurture her all those years as she had nurtured me. I wanted to tempt her, to feed her, to preserve her, to make her happy to be alive.

Certain situations would make me mindful of her. During the June '77 blackout in New York, when all the lights went out and people were stranded in unlikely places, I immediately thought of her. Alone in her dark apartment, vision so poor she'd barely be able to grope about, the elevator power out and she seven stories up, no water even for a cup of tea. Frightened perhaps. Did she have candles? Would she fall?

Moments of celebration included her. I'd call. Guess what? Sarah lost a baby tooth; Dan is opening an important new film; one of my stories has been accepted for publication; we're buying a summer house; Emily is playing in a concert—will you come?

Bella was often part of our plans: she was good company. On Sundays, it might be a movie matinee. Or on a weekday evening a professional preview, occasionally ill-chosen since it never occurred to us that some fare

might not be fit for Bella's consumption. Once, after a
pre-opening screening of *The Exorcist*, the publicity
director approached her, this kindly, elderly Jewish
lady, and asked out of curiosity: "Were you shocked by
the film?" "Nothing new," she shrugged. "It happened
in my village all the time, a young woman becoming
possessed by the dybbuk." She was visibly upset, however, by a play about young addicts and their disintegration, directed by our friend Jack Gelber. "*Nebech!*"
she resorted to Yiddish after the performance. "Young
lives destroyed." Art had the capacity to make her
suffer. Innocent of Aristotelian theories of catharsis, she
responded intuitively and totally. She took art seriously.
Was particularly moved by abstract painting. My
sister and daughter, both painters, valued her opinions.

Her vision, weakened by a glaucoma that dated to
the trauma of my sister's birth, deteriorated through
the years. At its onset, the doctors had operated on one
eye and warned her not to have more children. The
glaucoma in her second eye was kept stabilized by
drops and pills that reduced the eye pressure. In her
last year her pace slowed. She walked as if measuring
her steps through the geography of earth. She'd pause
at times to scan the way. It became hard for her to
read, to make out her bills. I signed her checks, paid
Con Edison, the telephone company, her rent, her Blue
Cross, her Medicare, her charities. Each month I cor-
roborated her existence, her abode, her needs, her participation. I was a parent testifying on behalf of a dependent. I signed her name.

Now her correspondence arrives directly at my mail-
box. Some of the letters I mark: Return to Sender.
Others I answer. *Shut out her lights,* I tell Con Edison.

Don't ring, I inform New York Telephone. Let her sleep. Do not disturb. Walk on tiptoe. My child is sleeping.

Her mail comes. A new form of junk mail from the monument merchants. We're on all their lists. A fresh outlet for their product. When pregnant, you're suddenly deluged with introductory copies of *Baby Talk,* brochures advertising maternity clothes, layettes, cribs, carriages, high chairs, walkers. Now we're on a new mailing list. This is a last purchase I must make for my mother. Granite, matchless granite the brochures call it, from Rock of Ages quarries at Barre, Vermont. Memorials guaranteed never to streak, fade, discolor, crack, or deteriorate. Motifs of Wild Roses, Menorahs, Laurels, Acanthus Leaves. There's also black marble. And Carrara. What would she have liked?

My sister and I select her last bed. There's a large selection to choose from. Mahogany, oak, cherry. Classic designs. Carved or unadorned. Her neighbor, Mr. Weinberg, the elderly Orthodox Jew, has advised me on the proper casket. Simple pine. He warns against a mafia of grave robbers. If you bury in lavish coffins, those mercenaries are apt to unearth the coffin the moment the family's back is turned, switch caskets, and sell the opulent one on the black market. He shakes his head. In America everything is a business. Then he shrugs. Nothing surprises him. He survived Dachau.

Twenty-eight years ago my mother accompanied me for the purchase of my wedding bed. French provincial it was, and cherry wood, in the going style for newly-weds of the fifties. It had matching pieces, a double dresser and bureau. It was her gift. You'll have it for life, she said. We didn't. In the sixties we switched to a king-size bed. But my mother did have her bed for life.

It was their wedding bed. The bed I was conceived in, and nursed in, the bed where I recuperated from measles, and scratched at chicken pox. It was the bed where she tended and comforted me. On days when I was sick I liked to crawl into it. I can still remember the old-fashioned scrollwork design on its headboard, the smell of its beech wood after she'd polished it with lemon oil, the pillows fragrant from their daily airings, that pale green goose-down quilt. It's the bed my father died in, and the bed my mother rose from on her last morning at home. It's the bed I must now give away. Will our eldest daughter perhaps want it in her new loft?

B<small>ELLA</small> had the most simple life, but not the most ordinary. She was born in the year 1904 in the small Galician town of Dynow, a part of Poland that then belonged to Austria. Her father was a wholesale butcher. His name was Nathan. He was a short, vigorous man with a dark beard and a clubfoot. On Saturdays, he liked to bring worshippers home from the synagogue for Sabbath lunch: the beadle, a kosher poultry man, beggars, an old widow from the poorhouse. Bella's mother was a tall, fair woman who wore her hair braided round her head. A pious Jewess, she covered it when going outdoors. My maternal grandmother's name was Toby, like mine. I never saw how she looked, since my mother had no photograph of her. There was one, however, of my grandfather. My mother was nine or ten when the war began and the Russians invaded their village. It was *erov shabbes*, my mother remembered, on the eve of the Sabbath. The Cossacks came tearing through the streets on horseback, heavy boots and flailing swords clattering against the walls of the houses. They swarmed in like wild, monstrous bugs. It was a nightmare, villagers shouting and wailing, goats and cows and horses shrieking and bellowing, chickens squawking, children weeping. Jews racing in all directions. *"Gevalt!"* cried a man. "They killed my wife." And her head was rolling in the street.

My mother's family fled south in a straw-filled cart carrying only a few possessions, some blankets, their candlesticks, the Sabbath hallah, cheese and apples. They headed south toward Hungary and Czechoslovakia. On the voyage, my mother was later to tell me, they often didn't have "from what to eat." En route, Bella's mother and an older brother died of cholera. The Black Death. She left her husband, a five-month-old infant, and four young children. Many refugees perished. Whole villages were disinfected.

After the war, the family returned to Dynow. For a whole year my mother did not speak. And she lost her hair. Sometimes she dreamed that her mother had returned to the infant and was stooping over the cradle to give her breast. But in the dream she could not stoop low enough. Two years later, the widowed father remarried through matchmakers a woman from the neighboring village. My mother was beside herself. "I'm a man," he tried to explain to her, "with five children and in business. Your grandmother's an old woman. She comes every day and helps us, but can't carry the responsibility of running our household."

My mother pulled a long face at the bride the moment she entered. The substitute for her mother. "That one," as she referred to her.

"Things were bad from the start," my mother told me in later years, "but when that one began having children of her own, I resented it terribly." In less than three years, the stepmother bore two children.

And then there was something else that rankled at my mother. Her father, upon remarrying, had given his bride several gifts—a ring, earrings, but, most galling of all, a gold chain. The chain, the traditional chattel a bride receives upon marriage—was the very one that had belonged to Bella's mother.

Every night, after her father's remarriage, Bella would go to her grandmother's to sleep. She didn't want the old woman to be alone, and besides, she hated everyone in her father's house. Holding a lantern, she'd stumble through the dark streets, muddy in spring, frozen and rutted in winter. At her grandmother's she stormed and wept, reporting the trespasser's latest violations, the daily favoritism shown her own children, the father's betrayal. The old woman, still grieving for her daughter, tried her best to calm Bella. "My daughter died. You lost your mother. It was God's will." Finally, realizing that her grandchild was irreconcilable and that bitterness blocked her future, she came up with a solution. "Go away, Bleemele, then you won't have to see or care what goes on in that house. You'll have a different life. A life of your own." "Where shall I go?" the grandchild asked. Going away evoked that nightmare flight from pogrom and war which had led the family to Hungary and Czechoslovakia, with her mother's death en route. The old woman pointed to two photographs of her other daughters which hung on the wall. "Go to them. To America. They'll treat you like a daughter."

Permission from her father, letters to America, and arrangements got under way. One morning, in the meantime, Bella came racing to her grandmother's house. Panting and sobbing. She'd seen *that woman* wearing the gold chain. The chain the little girl remembered hanging on her own mother's neck, beneath that sweet face with those rain-colored eyes and ash-blond plaits. Its burnished gold had illumined her way as she went about her everyday chores in their Polish village: sweeping, stoking the wood stove and baking bread, putting on the soup pot and throwing mushrooms inside, shelling peas, shining the copper kettle, nursing the baby, braiding Bella's hair, playing cat's cradle with Bella, handing her after school a thick slice of black bread with goose fat and salt. For ten years Bella's mother had worn that chain. True, her father had bestowed it as a wedding gift to the new wife, but it was one thing to own it, another for that witch to flaunt it on her neck! Until now, it had always been kept in a drawer. Nowadays, the only time she took it off was when she went to the monthly ritual bath—she should only drown! Seeing those gold links around the smooth, plump, hateful neck of the intruder, my mother wished that it were a noose. She wept bitterly to her grandmother. Even the old woman became riled. Better that the chattel be in her grandchild's possession than with a *fremde*, an outsider. "Look," she advised my mother, "if you really want to get the chain, there's a way. One day when the other one comes from the baths, tell her that you have some papers in the drawer which I need in order to send for your passport. And then . . ." My mother carried out the plot. No sooner did the stepmother unlock the drawer than Bella grabbed the chain and dashed out of the house. The stepmother ran and overtook her, whereupon Bella gave the woman a violent push that threw her to the ground, and then escaped to her grandmother.

The old woman kissed and hugged her grandchild. Meanwhile, the beleaguered stepmother was furiously recounting the whole story to her husband. My grandfather came at once to his mother-in-law's house. When he entered, Bella burst into tears. "Why are you crying?" he asked. "First, you take my wife's chain and beat her up, and then you cry?" Bella could not stop. Her body heaved with sobs. Patting her head, her father said softly, "If you had asked me for the chain in a nice way, I would have given it to you . . . it was your mother's . . . Come home."

"I won't go home," Bella told him. "I'll stay here." Her grandmother was crying, too.

"Give me the chain," said the father. "Before you leave for America, I'll return it to you."

But the grandmother spoke up. "She took it. She has it. So let it be."

And it was.

My mother never returned to her father's house.

When her boat arrived at Ellis Island, the chain was on her neck. For fifteen years after her arrival, it lay in a drawer. When I was thirteen and my sister ten, my mother took it to a jeweler, who made of it two bracelets, a double row of gold links interspersed with flat golden bars and joined at the center with an inscribed gold heart. I never wear the bracelet. It lies in my drawer. I'm afraid of losing it.

Bella's cousin took her to see Niagara Falls and then put her on a train to New York City. There she lived with the family of her mother's sister in a cramped apartment behind their grocery store on Third Avenue and Sixty-third Street. Soon after my mother

arrived, she sold her long black hair to a wig salon for
ten dollars and bought a red silk blouse with the money,
a red blouse with a tasseled belt. From then on, she
always wore her hair short. She found a job, first as a
milliner's assistant, eventually as chief hat designer. At
twenty-two, she married my father. He was ten years
older than she. An only son in a family of five daughters.
In Poland he had been a Talmudic scholar who spent
his days in the study house. He spoke Yiddish, Polish,
German, Russian, Hebrew, and Aramaic. His mother
was frail, his father improvident, fanatically religious,
and utterly eccentric.

When they came to this country, my father exchanged the study house for a window-cleaning route
to provide bread for his clan, which is how he earned
his living all his life. He always worked for himself,
never for a boss. He supported both families, his parents' and his own. Joseph was of medium height and
broad-shouldered. He had deep-set gray eyes with yellow glints, and light-brown hair parted on the side. His
thick eyebrows met over the bridge of a stern aquiline
nose. His cheekbones were high and prominent, almost
Mongolian. He was a hairy man and somewhat shy
about the exuberant growth on his forearms and chest.
After bathing in the sea, he always covered up with a
shirt. He had beautiful hands, with hair on the long
bony fingers. I share several of his features, the shape
of his hands, his deep-set eyes, as well as a certain quirk
he had of jiggling his right foot over the left crossed
knee. When I remember him, it is with hair that had
already begun to recede. He was a temperate man, didn't
smoke, drink, eat sweets, or use pills. Of simple tastes,
he relished the water potatoes were cooked in. He gave

us rides by letting us stand on top of his shoes while he strode around the apartment. He was a loving father and husband, a socialist in his early years and a follower of Eugene Debs, a practicing Jew until his father's death (at which time Joseph was in his fifties), not an especially sociable man, somewhat prudish, and a gambler. He had great veneration for education: wanted his children "to be somebody!" He spent the last sixteen years of his life a victim of Parkinson's disease, and the last five anchored to my mother's nursing. We all grieved when he died, though an outsider might have considered it a release from eventual total invalidism.

I did not look at all like her.

She was not tall, maybe five foot three or four. Her hair was charcoal-black, her eyes dark brown and very soft, with that air of human vulnerability you sometimes see in a Rembrandt painting. At times, she looked rather Japanese. Her nose was a bit wide. Her bosom full, her belly round, her rump flat. Her hands were strong, the palms wide, the fingers delicate and shorter than mine. She could knead dough and unscrew tight jars with great force. She loved to launder by hand, to get her hands wet as she put it, sudsing, scrubbing, wringing vigorously. Our house never lacked its box of Rinso and Ivory Snow. When displeased with my sister or me for some childish mischief, she deployed those hands for pinching us. A small specific pinch which telegraphed her anger. She never spanked.

Her body remained supple to the end. She stooped and rose briskly. Her legs were shapely and without varicosity, her neck unwrinkled, the skin of her body firm and white. She had splendid teeth, missed only one, the upper rear on the left.

As a young woman, she favored the color red. Later, the muted shades. In her thirties, she wore skirts and soft, tailored blouses, cotton or silk. When I learned to sew, at around twelve or thirteen, I would stitch these blouses for her, of men's shirting usually, in soft colors, sometimes stripes or a small print. I turned them out fast, had her pattern down to a science, became a shirt-waist virtuoso. One day I'd cut out two or three, stitch on the next, make buttonholes on the last. It gave me great pleasure. There was never a need for fittings, which both of us would have found tiresome. After each wearing, she laundered and starched her blouses. They dried on the clothesline and always smelled of the sun.

In later years she turned away from the confinement of skirt waistbands in preference for chemises and smocks in soft challis and jersey, the sort that became stylish in the early seventies, but which she had worn long before. Her preference ran toward pliant clothes, no stiffness, no starch. She did not wear a watch or jewelry. She had her own style, which did not deviate with fashion.

Her shoes had a medium heel and an open back. She wore her stockings rolled only halfway up her thighs and held with round elastics. When she took off her stockings, the imprint of the garters bisected her thigh. I used to chide her on cutting the blood circulation. She never paid attention. Did things her own way. She owned no garter belt. Hated constricting garments like corsets or girdles or tight brassieres. As soon as she came home, she'd throw off her shoes and clothes and get into a flowing cotton robe.

In the winter she wore tweed coats, but shed them at the first sign of spring. I remember certain hats of hers in the thirties, small soft hats with pointed brims that tilted over one eye in high milliner's style. Sometimes the hat had a feather. In later years, an Irish woolen lace scarf in mauve or heather might cover her head in January and February. She never used gloves, even in the cold. They seemed a hindrance between those powerful hands and the world. Umbrellas, another encumbrance. When Bella swam, it was with a sidestroke. A relaxed, untaught motion. Her head remained above water, her hair didn't get wet.

She drank her coffee much too hot, her soup too. She liked the heel of the bread, and the gizzard of the chicken. Had a great fondness for marrow bones. Her favorite dessert was cheesecake. Made with farmer cheese, so that it was light and not too rich. She liked coffee ice cream.

Her own cooking was simple and very tasty. She never cooked from a written recipe. Disdained gadgets. Wielded a primitive can opener which required that she lunge its point into the metal to gain entry. She sliced bread against the pressure of her thumb, beat egg whites with a fork, chopped onions and garlic with a handy paring knife.

When marketing, she sought out the freshest produce, the most perfect specimens, the choicest cuts of meat. Never comparison-shopped. At her table you tasted each ingredient, undisguised by sauces or gravies; salads were dressed with lemon juice and a sprinkle of cold water. The vegetables were cut in every which way for salad, and for soup, too. Her chicken soup was clear and fragrant with soup greens, a spray of parsley and dill tossed in at the end, the dumplings buoyant and fluffy. The sorrel soup in May was fresh and tart, the peaches stewed with sour cherries pink and perfumed.

She made pies with a well-baked buttery cookie crust, and corn muffins that were puffy and golden. Her coffee cake was rich with yeast, cinnamon, nuts and raisins, and the *pogacsa*, those sweet Hungarian yeast biscuits she'd learned how to make from an elderly Hungarian woman, melted in one's mouth. You always had to eat at least four. One could never cadge a recipe from my mother, since she cooked intuitively, didn't measure. If you asked for one, she'd offer instead to let you watch her do it. "I can't explain," she'd say. So you'd sit by the wooden kneading board and watch her pour the flour, make the well, add the eggs and the butter and sour cream and lemon and sugar. A little of this, a little of that. "The important thing is how you handle the dough. You have to knead thoroughly. Then bake well." If you questioned how long you had to knead, she'd reply, "It isn't a matter of time, you knead till it feels right." And you baked till it was golden. Her severest criticism for store pastries: "Raw dough."

I often think of her baking. The smell of yeast reminds me of her. Buds of yeast afloat in a half cup of warm milk sprinkled with sugar. Cells of yeast breathing, beginning to seethe and stir, gathering a ferment of life. I can picture her strong hands kneading, the maternal dough expanding. Resilient dough, fragrant and moist, taking shape. Living, leavened stuff springing from the heel of her hand as she pressed it, folded it, turned it. I can see the little indentation made with her second and third fingers to test the dough. It sprang back with a secret energy. Then she'd set it to rise in a warm, snug place, covered with a dish towel. From beneath the cloth came small percolating sounds, life sounds. Embryo of bread. When it had puffed to double its size, my mother brought it back to the kitchen table, dealt it a neat punch to restore it to original size, then shaped the loaves, twisted the rings, curled little coffee horns. Once more, these would be set to rise before entering the oven. For me, it was each time a transformation anew, that metamorphosis of flour into bread and cake. And my mother was the source.

Bella had no hobbies, nor was she a collector. She did not knit or do needlepoint. When she sewed, it was always by hand. She never operated our Singer sewing machine, or for that matter any washing machine, dryer, or dishwasher. Occasionally she'd stitch hats for us, a hangover, I suppose, from her millinery days, soft whimsical shapes of her own contriving from wool jersey lined in foulard silk, that clung to the head, or felt caps with pointed peaks. One summer she made a batch of granny caps from some printed calico, the sort worn in Victorian times to keep chills from the head. It was hard to figure an occasion to wear one of those funny caps. I wear mine at times in the country after washing my hair when the house is drafty.

Bella was not a gregarious woman. Dropping in on neighbors or passing the time in gossip was not up her alley. She had no patience for those old feminine topics —recipes, fashion, childrearing, husbands' infidelities. Even as a widow, she was not one of those ladies you see at Chock Full O'Nuts, hair coiffed silver-blue or ash-blond, who use the counter as their café, exchanging rumors and confidences, detailed recipes which substi-

tute margarine for butter, relaying the latest antics of
their grandchildren, the exploits of their children. She
was friendly but not outgoing. Did not boast about her
children or grandchildren. Secretly, she felt it was bad
luck. She was proud of our accomplishments, but her
pride was for home consumption. Like a favorite dish
you prepare only for family and not for company.

My mother had a certain hermitic quality. She did
not solicit friends or form close bonds with members of
her generation, the sort of ties one nourishes and re-
plenishes on a daily basis. Though she maintained telephone relations with a few former card-playing cronies
in which each kept up with the life of the other, she
never took the trouble to go uptown or downtown for a
visit, or to join one of them at a movie, a concert, a
restaurant, Bloomingdale's. On one or two occasions,
my mother-in-law, who dearly loved going places, invited my mother to embark on a trip with her, perhaps
share a winter vacation in the South. My mother de-
clined. For such a lively person, she had an astonishing
lack of curiosity about the world. Books, politics, travel
meant nothing to her. Her need for external stimulation
was altogether small. She resisted intrusions on her privacy, had small threshold for the steady companionship
of other women. Sometimes I wonder if her traumatic
childhood hindered the skill or inclination to form
close friends.

There was, however, one group activity in which she
did participate when she was younger. Card playing.
My father, too. In those days, when my sister and I
were growing up, my mother would go to afternoon
card games, women's games held at individual homes.
But there were also all-night floating card games held
in hotels, which they both frequented.

Bella played poker like a pro. With verve. She did not play recklessly, but was foxy. She watched the cards, studied the other players, knew when to bluff, when to pass, when to double. She was not timid at the table. She played to win. Unlike my father. He played as the gambler plays. The card game was a metaphor for those decisive upheavals that settle one's destiny. My father played to lose. It was that way in the stock market, too. He served as unofficial investment advisor for all of our relatives and for those friends of his who followed the ticker tape at the brokerage office on Eighty-sixth Street and Lexington Avenue. They were the beneficiaries of his scholarly porings over the blue books and his up-to-the-minute knowledge of the Dow Jones average. Their dossier held securities like American Tel and Tel, General Motors, General Electric—the blue chips. "Just put them away and forget about them," my father prudently recommended. His own investments were speculative, recondite, fly-by-night companies no one had ever heard of, Alaskan mining enterprises, Indonesian oil digs, purchased over the counter—on high margin—which he invariably sold before their breakthrough. He could have become rich many times had he held on to papers like IBM, Westinghouse, and certain burgeoning pharmaceutical companies. But that wasn't what he cared about. He played for risk.

For my father, gambling was a mania, and he was incorrigible. It was as if he were struggling with forces that oppressed him. A fanatic, perpetually bankrupt father, five dependent sisters, a hypochondriacal mother, relentless days of physical labor. The elemental sameness of his life. Each time he lost he wounded himself. Once, years later, after he had a devastating financial tailspin, a sister of his chided my mother for having failed to curtail him. My mother took to heart this criticism. But she could not stop him. No one could. During the Crash and Depression, when Western Union boys delivered telegrams at our door demanding that margins be covered, she implored, wept, cursed, but was not strong enough to curb that irrational force in him. In every other way he was a good husband.

The framework of Bella's life was simple. Uncluttered by the written word and received ideas. Though meagerly educated, she was highly intelligent and intuitive. More interested in humans than history.

She was a woman who took life seriously. Mindful that we're all mother's children, malleable and porous at birth, and all going to die. Bella was direct, disclosed, spiritually unveiled. You saw that nakedness of soul in her eyes. She knew the rare truths that the heart is capable of attaining directly.

One sensed that Bella had something to say. Like Edward G. Robinson, who claimed in *Double Indemnity* to be in touch with the "little man inside," Bella, too, was in touch with her "insides." She knew herself. Her views were not chewed-over lucubrations, received morality, concern with what people would say, what "they" would think, but derived from her own vantage point.

In her life, she was unapprehensive. Though twice mugged, she remained unintimidated in her movements, unlike many of the elderly in her building. One woman, always rouged, powdered, and dolled-up like a geisha for her daily Broadway promenades, trembled to

ride up in the elevator alone. The poor bedizened creature would stand in the doorway of her building till
someone she knew, maybe Bella, came along to accompany her up. Who knew what assailant might be lurking
inside with a knife or gun? Hadn't the eighty-four-year-
old father of Joe Rosen, a neighborhood merchant, been
stabbed on his way to the bank? Stabbed for eighteen
dollars. And hadn't seventy-eight-year-old Mrs. Adler
been thrown to the ground by an eleven-year-old mug-
ger, the cash from her Social Security check seized
from her handbag, her eyes sprinkled with Mace? You
couldn't blame anyone for being scared. Bella, though
not rash, did not glance back over her shoulder as she
walked home.

Always an outspoken person, she was unafraid of
confrontation. She had her opinions and did not tiptoe
amid ambiguities. Family squabbles never laid her low.
We were free to disagree, get angry, show our feelings.
One evening at the table, after dinner, she and my husband locked horns. They sprinted into skirmish,
barely shifting gears between disagreement and challenge. It wasn't my idea of dessert talk. I felt edgy over
the outcome of their sparring. Gingerly, I, peacemaker,
tried to inject a conciliatory note. Neither of them
would hear of it. They proceeded to shout at one another until their feelings had been aired like wash on a
clothesline. I wish I could remember what they were
arguing about. A half hour later, the two of them sat in
the living room, my husband puffing peacefully on his
cigar and laughing at a story Bella was telling with all
the juicy details of a novelist about the latest thumb-on-
scale trick pulled by the local kosher butcher. A *ganef*—
a crook—I heard her conclude from the next room,

---

where I had fled to some invented chore. My husband roared. Vaguely, I heard her say: "Danny, let's go gambling."

She had no use for liars and phonies. People who flashed a toothy smile but didn't say what they meant. People who beat around the bush and tried to get the best of you. She had a sharp nose for sniffing out flattery and hypocrisy.

Bella was generous. Liked to think of herself as "a sport." When you were with her, you felt her abundance. She didn't hold back in giving of herself or of her time, nor was she stingy in material matters. She took taxis with aplomb—having little patience to cue up for buses or be jostled by sardined bodies. She made purchases without pinching pennies, and played cards with style. Several times she loaned us her modest savings to embark on some new, often chancy, venture. She didn't curb her offspring with misgivings or cautionary tales. The best thing you can offer children, she believed, is hope. "Whatever you do, do the right thing" was her simple advice, thus giving us open field to make our own choices and pursue our inner demons.

Bella was affirming, encouraging, generous with praise. If you published a book, painted a beautiful canvas, launched a film, cooked a perfect soufflé, her compliment was invariable. "You deserve a medal." My mother gave out more medals than General Eisenhower. But somehow each time she awarded one, you heard it afresh.

In certain ways she was cautious. Had proper respect for the evil eye. Tied a red ribbon on our infant's crib to ward off Lilith—that witch malevolent to both mother and child and given to sudden apparitions in nursery and confinement rooms. Another tactic my mother had—this for an envious bystander—was with arm foreshortened to show a thumb through a clenched fist. Before flattery, she was silent.

When we were children, my mother was wary about making promises. A promise made was a promise kept. And who knew what trick destiny might have up its sleeve? Never disappoint a child, she believed. Never betray his faith.

Bella was not rigid. She accepted human frailty. To the excessive "social" drinker, she did not say, "Abstain." Cut down, was her advice. "If he enjoys a drink, why shouldn't he have a little one?" To the dieter, she'd offer a small slice of her freshly baked apple pie. She didn't have the heart to deprive people totally of their pleasure, or even of their weakness. It may in fact be true that she lacked the force to deny my father the card table—it was his great pleasure. In principle, she believed that you can kill with kindness, and in later years blamed herself for not having been tougher when it came to curbing his card playing and stock-market excesses. Who knows if she could have prevented him from gambling, from depleting their savings, from the forced sale of their insurance policies. She was grateful to my husband for his subsequent intervention in reorganizing their financial affairs, which included employing my father and her at the theater: she, as candy seller, he as sentry.

My mother was not a strict parent. She did not punish us. If ever she swatted us, it didn't hurt. It was the gesture. As a child, if I complained, on rising, of a sore throat, or feeling tired, or some slight indisposition, she'd encourage me to take the day off from school. "Rest," she said. "You'll be a teacher a day later!" She deprived me from the start of the stolen pleasure of playing hooky. Her lenience aborted truancy. In the early grades, I was often "tardy," but seldom absent. In other ways, too, her total acceptance precluded rebelliousness. What she didn't impose, I took it upon myself to enforce.

At times, if there was something she didn't want me to do and I pestered long enough, she'd wind up saying, "Do it, if you want it so much, do it." And that was all she need say. Suddenly fulfillment of my coveted outing or adventure rested squarely in my own hands. At which point I'd ask myself: Do I truly desire this so much that I'm prepared to upset her? Life seemed good or bad only insofar as my mother and father were happy or sad. In the end, I'd turn and walk off without a word, deciding more often than not against the escapade. Or, sometimes on the spot, I'd say, "I guess I'll forget about it if you're so against it."

Bella's greatest strength was her power of empathy. Hers was a spirit of pity which did not reject people for their weakness. *Nebech*, she'd say for the alcoholic, the junkie, the prostitute, for the lost souls. *A mama's kindt*, a mother's child!

Take the case of Francisco, the neighborhood drunk. A courtly Cuban gentleman of around sixty, once a successful restaurateur, now one of those anonymous, solitary dwellers in the disheveled brownstones on the side streets of the Upper West Side. Unable to work because of his drinking bouts, he'd hang around the theater when sober, do an occasional odd job, pour out his life story to Bella. Lucid and soft-spoken, he'd expand on his past, toss her *piropos*—verbal bouquets—in Hispanicized English in praise of her beauty, youthfulness, and character. Though totally innocuous, those conversations prompted dirty looks from my father, who, number one, had short shrift for alcoholics, and, number two, was totally possessive of my mother and jealous of any male overtures toward her. Francisco would make Bella laugh; she'd make him promise to go on the wagon. "You're such a fine man, so capable," she told him, "make up your mind to give it up." He promised, in all good faith he promised. For several days, a week, we'd see him clear-eyed, neatly dressed, raising his hat in greeting to familiar passersby, pinching the cheeks of friends' children, inquiring after everyone's health. Then, for a few days, he vanished. Only to show up red-eyed, unshaven, in rumpled suit, looking haggard and miserable. Dead drunk, or hung over. "*Nebech*," said my mother.

It was the Hebrew concept of *rachmones*, of pity or compassion. Interestingly, the Hebrew word *rechem*, from which *rachmones* derives, signifies "a mother's womb." Judaic ethics are imbued with the notion that one ought to look upon others with the love and feeling that a mother feels for the issue of her womb.

One of her friends was Dubby, a sometime porter at the theater. A tough-looking Harlem black who carried a shiv tucked in his sock, ran numbers for a living, and tended his invalided arthritic grandmother up on "Twenty-fifth," his nomenclature for 125th Street. He fed the old woman, bathed her, bought her a color TV. Dubby got around town on a Kelly-green bicycle. At times, after cleaning the theater, he'd bed down for the night on the paisley carpet, where we'd find him the next morning at an early screening. He was fiercely devoted to my husband, warned him of any fishy character who might be casing the joint for a stickup, and once or twice phoned in the middle of the night to complain in four-letter mother-fucking talk about some uppity blacks who were installing new seats during his shift. His mother, Zelda, was a slender, soft-spoken woman who day in and day out propelled a steam iron in the back room of a local dry cleaner.

Whenever Dubby passed the New Yorker, he'd drop by to shoot the breeze with Bella. She dug his black language and intuitively understood it, metaphors and all. "He's a nothingness," Dubby would say disdainfully about Paul, the assistant manager at the theater, a starched managerial type who did his shift decked out like an undertaker in black serge, white on white shirt, and patterned gray silk tie, trying, unsuccessfully, to inject a note of formality in the incorrigibly informal cinematheque atmosphere of the New Yorker. Bella laughed. Secretly she agreed. "Maybe he's a nothingness, but he tries to do his job." Dubby shrugged. "Uh-huh, that honkie man got a head worsen a water hydrant," or he'd address himself to Paul's Irish nose, which in his view was just like a car fender. Dubby studied Paul scrupulously, every detail, and one day, noting a pair of new patent-leather shoes, complimented him with feigned innocence and a note of irony unmissed by even stolid Paul: "Man, them shoes say M-M-M!" Clearly they were not kindred souls. Eventually Dubby's provocations provided him with his walking papers, but no hard feelings, eh?, he told my husband. Dubby continued to visit Bella. In those days in the sixties, when many blacks adopted Afros and dashikis, Dubby never veered from his chinos and short haircut. "Maybe they got Afros on their heads, but they don't recollect they black in their skin." "I tell you, Bella," he said once. "Everything is everything." Bella quoted him as if he were Ben Franklin. One day, he came and told her: "I don't have to run numbers no more." He never mentioned what activity was replacing his original pursuit. Bella didn't ask. Months later, he showed up at the theater in tears. His grandmother had died. In her sleep. "She just passed on like a little angel," Dubby said. Bella comforted him. "Everything is everything," she said to Dubby.

Young people sought Bella out. They could confide their worries, their transgressions, the misunderstandings with their families. Though she was of an alternate generation, of a time when girls were virgins till marriage, when young people didn't smoke pot or drop acid, when white girls didn't date black boys, when students didn't drop out, or take trips to India, these things didn't make her faint. She believed that things can change with good will. She listened, expressed her opinions freely, disapproved without beating around the bush. Gave counsel.

It was that way when I was young. At age ten, when I came home and excitedly told her about the man in Bronx Park who had unzipped his fly for my delectation and showed me the most amazing thing, my mother, unabashed, promptly relayed all there was to know about the nether parts. She was not squeamish about forbidden subjects, feminine topics. Menstruation was conveyed to me as an event to be welcomed. You were a woman. Being a woman was terrific.

Bella liked to engage in physical play, pinch our daughters puckishly on their arms, little nips like a bird pecking at choice morsels of suet. She also enjoyed "a little tickle." In turn, each of the girls arrived at that proud moment when they were able to lift their grandmother off her feet. It was a turning point, having sufficient strength to raise her from the ground. Once Nina lifted her and squeezed her so hard, my mother had a sore rib cage for weeks. For the next couple of months, each time Nina approached, my mother backed off, properly cautious.

Bella was playful and witty. She understood the meaning of play in its life sense, and in games, too. My daughters loved to play cards with her. They played for money, to make it more interesting; a game requires stakes to generate risk. Though currency never appeared on the table, the girls kept detailed written records of how much each owed the other. Their games served as backdrop, like a weaver spinning, for other interplay, the kidding, tricking, peeking, accusing, cheating, bluffing—and recapitulating. My mother would spin tales about past triumphs at the card table —oh, those flushes and straights!—and also about the picaresque characters who circled bygone tables.

Eventually, she'd slam down the cards and declare: "No more." "Just one more!" the girls inevitably begged, and there'd be another hand, another round. And again they'd implore, "Just one little one more." They were insatiable. At last the final game was dealt and the four of them moved into the kitchen to brew a pot of tea. Imperceptibly, the camaraderie of the game slipped into the intimacy of sheer talk, a shuttling back and forth of exchanged anecdotes, jokes, confidences on their part, memories on hers, secrets, familiar cues and signals. They, like I, knew most of her stories by heart but were continually nourished by them. About how she'd come to America and slept in a bed squeezed between three beefy young nephews in back of her aunt's grocery store. About the bedbugs she'd unearthed when idly picking at the seam of the wallpaper in her cousin's apartment on Avenue C, where my mother lived a brief while. About Antwerp, where, be-

fore boarding the boat for America, she'd wired a tele-
gram to her aunt in New York asking for twenty-five
dollars, which she promptly spent on an irresistible red
dress seen on a mannequin on the main street of
Antwerp. After all, Bella wanted to arrive in New York
in style! I'd hear my daughters whispering, giggling,
chortling at old jokes they never tired of hearing, re-
peating over and over one of her Yiddish expressions to
catch the perfect intonation. *Brains, you can't buy
brains at the butcher's. That stupid man is a piece of
horse. The eye is small, yet it sees the world.*

So. What did Bella's life mean to her? Orphaned of
mother when very young, deprived of education, uprooted from birthplace and native tongue, she arrived
in this country alone. At her death, she left ten intimates who cherished her, who had the privilege of wit-
nessing her life. Ten descendants who knew her lines,
her gestures, her expressions, her phrases, her repertory
of anecdotes and memories, her pies, her soup, her
walk, her smell. And her generous smile. To ten people
she implicitly and relentlessly said: "In life there are
eternal problems, but you will deal with them."

And then there were others. The young people, unre-
lated to her, who observed her example and felt her
impact, the film buffs who bought candy from her at
the candy stand, the poker players, the merchants, the
neighbors, all of whom had a strong sense of her. No
Margaret Mead, not an Eleanor Roosevelt, or a Simone
de Beauvoir, but a plain, strong woman who showed
that even an invisible life is worth living.

One of the people who knew her well was my friend
Judy. A close friend, the kind you have for twenty
years in a city not noted for lasting friendships, where
people drop in and out of your life as you change

neighborhoods, jobs, boyfriends, politics. Judy is one of those friends you may not see for weeks, months, or a year at a stretch if one of you goes away, but no sooner are you together than you pick up the strands of your ongoing dialogue. You're comfortable with her at any hour, in any attire, in any mood. She's the sort of friend who phones excitedly to tell you her good news, or to say, "Can you come over now? Tonight I'm afraid." The sort of friend who gives you gold stars and is not afraid to accept them from you.

At one period, while in the throes of a painful divorce, Judy on some evenings would come over and find Bella with us. Slowly recovering from the anguish, the anger, the disillusion of that marriage, Judy was regaining her confidence, her appetite for life, tentatively wetting her feet in a new job, relationships—even eating with appetite. At times, I used to think that the warmth she showed Bella stemmed from our friendship, but in fact I now know that was not so. Judy could speak freely to Bella, laugh with her, relate to her. Bella gave sympathy, but not gloomy maudlin pity. Predictably, she encouraged Judy in an old-fashioned way to "find yourself a nice man." One fine day Judy announced in our living room that she was more than mildly attracted to someone in his late sixties. I threw up my hands in horror. Imagine, a beautiful, voluptuous woman in her early forties tying up with an old man, imminently ready for the geriatric ministrations of a Florence Nightingale. Ridiculous, I told her flatly. Stop looking for a father figure. Find someone of your own generation, a man with vitality, sexiness, a future, blah, blah! I could hear my plodding self, a nonstop record, adapting a conventional stance, ranting like a nudging mother. "But he *is* vigorous," Judy protested. "Besides,

I feel comfortable with him. He likes the things I do. He's a music lover. He makes me feel good about myself. He's gentle." I rolled my eyes, waiting expectantly for her to cite Pablo Casals, Picasso, Arthur Rubenstein, all those giants who achieved creative zeniths in their seventh decade. She didn't. My mother took a different view. "You can't plan for the future. If you like him and he's a nice man and you feel happy with him, I see nothing wrong." Judy beamed, suddenly reassured that she was not queer, a willful child striking out at wrong choices. "Bella, you're an angel. You understand." I continued to play the devil's advocate, but when Judy, bright-eyed, kissed us good night, I knew my mother was right. Maybe Judy would settle down with this comfortable man, maybe she wouldn't. Meanwhile, Bella had reinforced her faith in herself.

Bella knew how to build you up and she also knew how to make light of certain contretemps so that they didn't seem a tragedy. I remember one incident that happened when I was around nine. Our family was paying a Sunday visit to my mother's aunt, Tante Molly, and Uncle Moe. These were the grocery folk with whom Bella had lived when she arrived in this country. When we reached my aunt's house, at around three, Uncle was out, gone for a walk, my aunt told us. He'd be back any minute. We gave her the box of chocolates we'd brought and she served us coffee and honey cake. We sat around her mahogany dining table with its stern buffet and bowl of wax fruit—all my relatives seemed to have their respective bowl of wax fruit. The afternoon waned, the light faded outside. Meanwhile, Molly's three sons returned home, three husky, red-cheeked young men who were all attending City College to train for specific, secure jobs that would ascend them on the immigrant ladder, insulate them against depressions, assure them of not being grocery owners like their parents. One, in horn-rimmed glasses, aspired to be a CPA, another a pharmacist, the third would "sell"—he was studying business. The dinner hour approached and passed. Still no Uncle Moe. By now, my aunt was openly worried. She voiced fears of an automobile accident, a heart attack, all those things Jewish wives and mothers imagine when husbands don't return on time. My mother and father reassured her. Maybe he'd run into a friend or lost himself in a game of chess or . . . But soon they too looked worried. My sister and I sat on the rug playing checkers. The younger son set the table. My aunt halfheartedly warmed the pot roast and began washing lettuce. Suddenly the phone rang. It was the police station. Was she the wife of a white-haired, mustached gentleman of about sixty, dressed in a dark gray coat with a beaver collar and a felt hat? My aunt's face turned pale as she answered affirmatively. Well, the officer told her, this elderly gentleman had just been arrested in the Bronx Zoo for molesting a young woman. Would someone from his family come down to sign the papers for his release? The two eldest sons went. In their absence, my aunt tore her hair, cursed the day she met that good-for-nothing husband of hers, bemoaned her humiliation. My sister and I stopped playing checkers. My father, a prim, unrelenting moralist, didn't know what to say in front of the good woman. Secretly, he agreed with her. My mother took a different tack. "Look," she said, "thank God he's alive and in no danger. Calm down. Let's wait until he gets home and hear his side of the story. Who knows what really happened?" At last, a key turned in the door. The prodigal father, that splendid dignified-looking gentleman in the Borsalino hat and fur-trimmed coat, returned in the escort of his two sons. Shamefacedly, and in a low voice so that we children couldn't hear all the details, he spelled out the story. It had been a balmy day, so he decided to take a long walk in the zoo. While standing in front of the monkey cage, he noticed a fine-looking young woman who happened to be in the company of a young sailor. The lass was irresistible, the air bracing and infectious, and a free Sunday made you feel so free that, responding to impulse, he pinched the young lady's bottom. The miss let out a scream. "It's him, he pinched me," she screeched to her boyfriend. The sailor, properly defending his girl, his honor, and the U.S. Navy, grabbed the old man by the lapels and began insulting him, shouting so loudly that a cop came along. And the next thing, poor Uncle Moe found himself in the station house before a severe judge.

"*Oy vay iz mir,*" lamented my aunt, pinching herself and then flailing out at Moe. Such *shanda*, such shame. She was wild-eyed, my uncle looked one third his size. Even his usual bustling mustache was droopy.

"It's not so terrible," said my mother. "Could be worse. What did he do? He saw a tempting young woman, and he reached out to touch her. A normal man. What can you expect? Such a fuss. He loves you," she told my aunt, "you love him. *Kik avek.*" Look away.

The storm blew over. We all ate pot roast and had stewed prunes with apricots and tea. As we were going home on the Gun Hill trolley, I wondered what Tante Molly was doing to Uncle Moe. I could imagine her chasing him around the house, throwing the wax fruit at him, calling him names, reducing him forever by a peg. From then on, I could never look at Uncle Moe in the same way, even though in my mother's eyes it wasn't so *geferlich*, so terrible. You had to take people's pranks with a grain of salt. In fact, I had a feeling that maybe Moe rose a peg or two in her esteem. He became more human, more playful.

Legal formalities. Go to the vault, bids the lawyer, for your mother's papers.

I walk along Broadway, always with that absurd notion that I can run into her. She liked to sit on the island of benches between the uptown and downtown lanes. Preferred it to the park on Riverside Drive. People were more interesting than trees.

Broadway, in the eighties and nineties, is the dividing line between the good and bad sides of the tracks. It is the marketplace of the West Side, its promenade, its movie strip, its freak show, its avenue of the quotidian, the boulevard where residents meander and prowl, where the neighborhood pours its guts out. Balzac would have had a field day here.

Pick any day to watch other lives go by. A mother in young bloom pushing her rosy baby in his carriage, an ashen schizophrenic walking and talking to himself, gourmets emerging from Murray's and Zabar's, shopping bags bulging with smoked Nova Scotia salmon, paté, Camembert and chèvre, an itinerant bag lady scavenging for additions to her mobile hoard. You see schoolchildren munching pizza, and painted hookers stationed at their posts like faithful sentries. Glazed-eyed addicts totter past mink-clad matrons. A nubile fourteen-year-old, eyes averted but popping with curiosity, sneaks past a transvestite who has lifted his skirts to pee openly in front of the Korean fruit store. Elderly

Europeans, kinfolk of Isaac Bashevis Singer, and Singer
himself, stroll along, arms linked, discoursing on the
Holocaust, Spinoza, the rising price of bread.

Sometimes I'd spot my mother sitting alongside one
of these West Side characters. She lived on Ninetieth
Street but chose Eighty-ninth as her spot, perhaps because it provided a vantage point on the New Yorker
Theater between Eighty-eighth and Eighty-ninth. Also,
it faced Benny's Luncheonette, a neighborhood nexus.
The bench on Eighty-ninth Street had its habitués. An
old woman in sneakers who came every day at the same
time to read the *Racing Form* before scurrying down
the block to cast her ballot at Off-Track Betting. A
sooty vagrant, one of the West Side have-nots, drinking
beer or dollar sherry from his paper bag. A sprawling
black woman in her mid-fifties eating a Danish in the
sun while awaiting her grandson's dismissal at three
from P.S. 144 down the block. A rheumy Irishman, old
and frayed, a single-room side-street dweller, slowly
eating his roll and looking sad. There was also a faithful
coterie of dolled-up widows who used the bench as
their café. And perhaps a young mother spooning
frozen yogurt alternately into her child's mouth and her
own. From across the street, I'd watch my mother absorbed in the way the child automatically opened his
mouth in anticipation of each approaching spoonful.
Sometimes someone struck up a conversation with
Bella, the way people do when you sit down on the
verge of their lives.

Other times, she simply watched the West Side pro-
cession, a man carrying shirts to the laundry, people
emerging from the supermarket with laden wagons, the
blind man who lived on her block fearlessly crossing
the street and flaunting his cane like a baton, an elegant

woman in pince-nez tossing bread crumbs to the pigeons, the Fuller Brush man, who nodded to her as he purposefully strode past.

Today I cross the street when the light changes and stand by her bench. The light turns red. When it again flashes green, I move. Past the tuxedo-rental store with its sign: YOU GET MARRIED ONLY ONCE. Not these days, you don't. That legend is from Grandmother's days, as my mother might put it. The only thing you do once is get born and die. I walk on. Past Pick & Pay, the twenty-four-hour food store, past the photography studio, its window gallery filled with portraits, people dressed up for weddings, confirmations, bar mitzvahs, young girls delicate as cameos, knobby fiftieth-anniversary couples beaming at their accomplishment.

At last, the bank. The custodian admits me into the barred sanctuary of the vault. I sign my name to gain access to her strongbox—my mother kept the box in both our names—then stand alongside the vault keeper as he removes the metal box from its niche. The vault has a mortuary air. The guardian encloses me and the box in a tiny room with a lock on its door. The box is a small archive of my mother's life: her marriage certificate, citizenship papers, Medicare and Social Security papers. And, at the bottom, a tiny black-hinged box lined with purple velvet. Inside, the glitter of a diamond. Her engagement ring. She never wore it. "Who needs a flashlight for muggers?" she used to say. It is all there. All except the death certificate.

I empty the contents into my purse, witness the return of the strongbox to its niche, wait to be ushered out. On the other side of the barred gate stands an old woman, overly bundled up on this unseasonably warm day. A wool-jersey turban circles her head, thick stockings sag on her spindly legs. She is coming to her safe-box. To arrange her documents.

There was a time when I was strong. Active. Supportive. Nurturing. Possessed with that feminine desire "to be good." Jogging and chattering along, fascinated by the people on the street. Sound as an apple. Now I am anxious, pessimistic, indentured to death. I feel indifferent, powerless, unnurturing. I don't want to be needed, and indeed feel unneeded. As a mate, mother, or friend. My everydayness has snapped and I am in quarantine from the world. Want nothing from it, have nothing to give to it. When things get bad, the whole world is lost to you, the world and the people in it.

When I teach, I teach only words. Empty verbs stripped of meaning, conjugations bereft of person, participles dangling on blackboards without auxiliaries. Let the students decipher their own meaning in the babble I transmit. We all talk too much, read too much anyhow.

Existence is a burden. And I, an orphan. Orphan, from the Greek *orphanos*, a child whose parents are dead. Derivations and terminations. Any questions, class? Questions, questions. Ontological questions, metaphysical questions. What are bodies for? What's the meaning of creation? Of death? Such prattle! Only one truth, one reality, commands my attention. Life is a white shadow, death a dark shadow. Night, death, stillness, isolation, solitude: that is being. To be alive, to be urgent and insistent—those are mere delusions.

Sometimes she kidded me for my relentless activity. Stop running, she'd say. And my husband would chime in, nicknaming me the Mexican Jumping Bean. "Slow down," called out a good-natured construction worker one day as he saw me racing past as he sat on the sidewalk eating a hero sandwich for lunch. Well, that drumming energy is gone now. I want only to stay close to home. Away from events, community, participation, social traffic. At home, I feel closer to myself, free to think of her, undistracted. Did my momentum require her?

On the way home from class, I pass an elderly couple strolling arm-in-arm. He wears a beret and fur-collared coat. She, sturdy oxfords and a tweed of my mother's liking. His hand as they walk rests on his wife's shoulder. An ordinary West Side scene which triggers off that familiar knot in my throat, and tears. I continue on, crying, with the freedom of the anonymous weeper in New York. Halfway home, someone takes my elbow. I look up. It's Francisco.

"Oh, *señorita*, I'm so sorry. Bella was such a good person. *Una buena persona.* Character, she had character. May her soul rest in peace. But you must not carry on this way. It does not allow her spirit to rest."

I gaze up at Francisco and shake my head, too choked to muster speech. Today, he's clear-eyed and sober, his face filled with compassion. "You look good, Francisco," I finally say.

"I'm on the wagon. No more drinking."

"That's good, Francisco," I say softly, and walk on.

Why, you're behaving like a child, people might say, shaking their heads. Keep busy, someone advises. The only remedy is to distract yourself. Think of your blessings. Good health, a loving husband, fine daughters, demanding work. Time heals.

The pain of childhood, of disillusion, of loss, of death. If we don't touch the scars, pick at them, our history too disappears. As with one of those slates children draw upon that is covered with a transparent sheet which when lifted obliterates the past. We distract ourselves into oblivion. Our bruises, our blows, the places where branches were lopped off or pruned normalize and vanish into the body of tissue, and soon we barely remember where blood flowed and tears fell. As they say, a parent does not die till his children forget him. Soon we can say with aplomb: Time heals, life goes on, my life does not need yours.

But no. It isn't so. She's dead. And I'm dying. For near fifty years, we trod the same earth together. Two-thirds of my trajectory traversed, two-thirds of hers shared. The last third I must go alone, parentless, as my children, in turn, eventually must. One life is a continuation of the next. It's like one of those problems you find in math primers. If A=B−25, and B has traveled 75 miles, how many miles has A traveled? How many miles does A yet have to travel to cover a total distance of 75 miles?

I force myself to stare into the mirror. I see images of me as a child, as a corpse. I do not see myself as I am now. A corpuscle in the midst of its trajectory. Maybe

I'm almost dead. Oh, Mother, I've lost my reflection, my mooring, my roof. My map.

A single person is missing and the whole world is empty.

How to soften the pain of upheaval.

Making love, the supreme remedy for anguish: To make love is to plunge into the world prior to birth, prior to the great separation. To unite and reunite, to generate birth and be reborn. It is to find again that deep slowness, that wordless rhythm, that tidal dissolve. Darkness. Silence. Time suspended. Flesh unto flesh. Breath unto breath. My ear upon my husband's heart ausculates the steady beat of life. An ongoing world swelling, balancing, merging light with shadow, touch and dream. He curls around me. I become part of his smell. Two bodies entwined, throbbing, melting into a primal cocoon. Making love is the great regression. The great reunion. Blood, sweat, sperm. Birth, copulation, death. A race, a shared frenzy. Air rushing into the lungs. Quivering fire. A spasm of existence.

A detail: the pink laundry slip in her handbag.

She'd mentioned it her second day in the hospital, a Wednesday it was. I'd come to visit after class, and it was on her mind. She was attentive and orderly about household items. Her rent was paid on the first of the month, telephone and electricity bills were never overdue, doctors and dentists received their fees as soon as their hands were off her.

"Take the slip from my bag and pick up the laundry,"

she said. I laughed and replied, "It won't run away."
She didn't remind me again.

Weeks later, I descend the dark, steep iron steps
leading to the basement Chinese laundry. One of those
old-fashioned family-run laundries that you can still
find in the city. The owner and his wife, their young
son, and a white-haired grandmother live behind the
store. The odor is unmistakable—the same that I remember from childhood when I'd go to our neighborhood Chinese laundry. The proprietor, an illegal immigrant whose wife and children had remained behind,
stood behind the counter from daybreak to midnight
wielding his heavy iron. On the wall facing him hung
calendar pinups of Western women. I used to love to go
and pick up the wash and watch him add and subtract on
his abacus. He gave me lichee nuts and spoke at length
in singsong, syncopated English, substituting *l*'s for *r*'s.
But, more interesting, rumor had it that he was an extremely rich man, had hoards of money stashed away
amid the folded laundry, and that he had, to boot, a
beautiful blond Jewish mistress. I used to worry about
his left-behind wife. Wasn't he ever going back to
China? He never mentioned sending for her. That
steamy smell of sprinkled wash and starch yielding its
vapors to the sizzling iron is the same smell that permeates my mother's Chinese laundry.

The old woman, the owner's mother, dressed in a
black high-collared tunic, gray-haired and with a bun,
is sorting tickets when I enter. In the back, the wife is
stirring a pot. The fragrance of chicken broth and bok
choy combines with the Chinese laundry smell. The
child, a bright-eyed boy of about eight, is writing at a
table alongside the ironing board, sharing the table's
surface with some pressed and folded shirts. Other

ironed shirts are draped over a door for thorough drying before folding. The father, maybe forty, is ironing. I
appear at the counter, holding the pink ticket. He
leaves his iron.

Glancing at the ticket, he scrutinizes me as if unable
to reconcile my face with this number 247. Is it possible
that he knows every single one of his customers? That
he can identify every number with its retriever? My
mother used to describe how he'd carry her package to
the top of the steep, narrow dark steps, and once even
walked her to the corner of West End Avenue. The
store owner locates her package wrapped in its brown
paper and bound with narrow white cord and the typical bow so easy to untie. It's a large bundle.

I pay and turn to the door, holding my mother's last
parcel of laundry. She'd been coming here every other
week for eighteen years. Can I allow such a habitual
act to end without a word, without an explanation? You
have commerce with neighborhood merchants for years
and years. They get to recognize you, greet you, engage
you in talk about the weather. You watch their business
grow, and on some days their smiles relieve your loneliness, you exchange small talk uncomplicated by
troubles, you share a sense of community. Then suddenly a customer stops coming. "Whatever happened to
that friendly lady who had trouble seeing her way
down and up the dark steps?" the Chinese laundryman
might ask his wife. "You know, the one with the soft
eyes."

I turn back. The man is already halfway back to the
ironing board. He glances up quizzically. Had he given
me the wrong change? "Remember that elderly woman
with short, wavy hair and weak eyes?" I ask. "The one

you used to help up the steps?" Oh yes, of course he does. His eyes light up. "Yes, yes, nice lady." "Well, she died. It was my mother. And she died." "Oh, velly solly!" he exclaims. His wife and child and mother look up. His wife says something in Chinese. He turns and explains. She echoes his exclamation. The old woman looks sad. I go on: "She always used to say such nice things about you. That you were a kind man. That you helped her. I want to thank you, to thank you for my mother." He nods his head wordlessly, and a soft humming sound comes from his lips, like the sound a small animal or a bird might make.

Clutching the unwieldy package in both arms—how did she ever manage?—I pick my way up the steps and into the street. At home, I undo the string, fold back the brown paper. Inside are four sheets, six pillowcases, seven bathroom towels, and five dishtowels. Crisp, clean, and smelling fresh, ready to be used again.

I phone my sister. There are papers for her to sign, and my mother's engagement ring to give her. My mother, a few times, worried aloud to me because there was only one diamond ring, and how could you divide that in half? "Don't bother me with your diamonds," I'd banter when she raised the subject. "Maybe I should buy a second one," she went on, thinking aloud and ignoring my remark. "Terrific idea," I rejoined, "considering that you never even wear that one." "I know, but . . ." "Give it to Rozzie with my blessings."

My sister suggests that we meet at my mother's bench during the lunch hour. I arrive first. As she approaches, she seems smaller, and though the day is unseasonably warm, her head is bundled in a kerchief. She walks gracefully, boots turned out like a dancer, which she never was; maybe the habit took root during all those youthful years practicing the cello. Our faces merge, gray smiles cross over a kiss. I feel a teardrop on my hand. Hers? Mine?

Here, at Bella's spot, she places her signature on several documents, the papers required by law to de-institutionalize a parent. I hand her the little velvet box that contains the ring. She tucks it into her purse without opening it. "Mama wanted you to have it," I tell her. "I never wear diamonds," she says softly. "Hold on to it." She nods.

We sit silently, each gazing into space, the sun baking our backs, memories swirling like the deep swirl of the sea. In a while words come . . . She would have enjoyed a day like this . . . How are you doing? . . . How are the children? . . . The lump in my throat, the knot in my stomach are little padlocks on the outpourings that could rush forth unrestrained. My sister, my poor sister. But it's too early for consolation; my grief can only feed hers. My sister. Once we were so close, we whispered in bed, munched pretzels under the blanket, giggled under the summer slipcovers of the big dining-room table, threw cherry pits and corncobs from the fire escape, gorged on watermelon on steamy July nights, played go-fish and casino and built card houses, had mumps in adjoining beds, tested each other for spelling, poured plaster-of-Paris masks one for the other, told each other to shut up, snapped pictures of one another in tunics and Isadora Duncan poses, eavesdropped on each other's interminable phone conversations with boyfriends. We took our first steps one alongside the other. And now that our mother is gone, how will it be?

Was she our needed link? Will grief bring us closer, or draw us apart? One thing I know; I know how my sister hurts.

Damp, chill days of March, early-evening darkness, sooty ruffles of snow piled on sidewalk curbs and bus stops. Too cold to walk home from class, I stand at the kiosk and wait for the number 104 bus. It comes at last. I take the first seat by the door.

Facing me across the aisle is a disheveled woman with a bundled-up baby cradled on her lap. The thought of the child's coziness warms me. The woman is clearly oblivious to everything except the cherished creature on her lap. She rocks the child, hums and croons to him, and every once in a while lowers her face and nuzzles the unseen form.

One day they will separate, this mother and child. What will be the child's memories? Will he remember the mother in some typical pose, or in some idiosyncratic moment? Will he remember the bars of his crib? His mother leaning over the high chair or bath? Or telling a bedtime story? Or her silhouette in the dark? Or spanking him? Surely, the child will have no recall of her adoration as they rode uptown on the number 104 bus one cold March evening.

Suddenly my thoughts are interrupted by a small flurry of activity across the aisle. A new passenger in a green wool hat has seated herself alongside the adoring mother and, curious to have a peek at the hidden infant, sidles up close. She peers over the mother's shoulder toward her lap. Brusquely, and with a look of rage, the mother recoils, encircling her charge like a vigilant lioness whose cub is endangered. Meticulously, she rearranges the folds of the blanket, closing the opening, eliminating any possibility of the stranger casting her prying eye on the baby. The newcomer raises an eyebrow and grimaces smugly but makes no comment. At the next stop, the mother, holding her baby, hastily rises and gets off. The bus moves on.

The woman in the green hat, snickering, shoots me a conspiratorial glance. Leaning across the aisle, she stage-whispers behind cupped hand. *"The blanket was empty. There was no baby inside!"* Her toothy smile broadens.

Oh, how my heart opens to that deranged woman with her phantom baby, a woman longing for a child, a child longing for a mother.

W̲e go to Seville.

A belated journey. An oceanic voyage, a way of replenishing the energy and enthusiasm to go on in the world. Travel, a traditional means to recover from loss, disappointment, grief. The notion that in a foreign country, in a different language, the hurt will be less.

At the airport I cry: all those people bidding each other goodbye, happy, hopeful, confident that they'll be restored to one another. At takeoff I cry: our plane abandoning the earth and her body. At arrival in Spain I cry: the sight of welcoming families crowding the gates to greet arriving passengers. A baby is passed over the gate by a young couple into the waiting arms of jubilant grandparents. The grandparents seize the child and smother him in kisses.

We stay at a hotel opposite the cathedral and the adjacent Giralda. At every hour and half hour our walls

vibrate to the clang of the Moorish bell tower. The sun
shines all the time. Orange trees and palms bloom in
the streets. In the old Jewish quarter, blinding-white
houses lean toward each other in escape from an African
sun. Men with Arab faces squint against its rays. Glass-
enclosed balconies, grilled windows, pigeons nesting in
the grillwork, terra-cotta pots bursting with gerani-
ums break the white façades. Narrow streets magnify
your voice, and you hear the echoes of invisible voices
around invisible bends. In the morning we awaken to
the lackadaisical rhythms of a foreign city. Hoofs clattering in the streets, the shuffle of feet, voices laughing
and calling to one another.

In a hole-in-the-wall tobacco shop on the Giralda
side of the square, we sight a toothless old crone who
has seemingly forgotten her age, and also her inhibi-
tions, as she jokes with the habitués. A local wag in-
forms us that she's a hundred and one years old. Her
skin is like a leathery apple that has wintered on a
shelf. Her sparse gray hair has settled into a small top-
knot on the crown of her head. Her clothes are a rusty
black. The body, though crooked as an olive tree, is still
spry. And she is noisy. Like a jovial Halloween witch,
she chases one of the young men with a broom. He
screeches like a child in a game of tag. Her Spanish is
sheer Andaluz, syncopated, consonants dropped. Her
toothless mouth shouts out laughed warnings. Her time
hasn't come.

Palm Sunday. Twilight. Mary, borne tri-
umphantly on resplendent floats, through the city's
winding streets. The iron balconies are like teeth smiling. Scores of these *pasos* weaving through the city,

swaying and balancing above invisible human bearers. For hours, the crowd trails them.

At last, a float approaches its destination, its sheltering church. My husband and I stand amid the throng that has collected outside. It is dark. Light emanates solely from the tapers on the float and from the reflected radiance of the bejeweled and garlanded Virgin. The multitude of human bodies is massed together without barrier. Slowly, the iron doors of the church swing open on their ancient hinges. The float reenters its haven. As the door closes, a voice from some balcony overhead pierces the hushed black night with a dirge, a *saeta*, literally an arrow. You feel upon you the exhalation of human breath but hear only that one mournful human voice. An oratorio of sound. Its modulations and trills are Arabic, Semitic. For me a Kaddish.

Each time I left on a trip during my father's last years, he would say, "I probably won't see you again." It was his terrible cry of wolf. Yet one day he'd be right. I'd return and he'd be gone. He died, in fact, while I was one hundred miles away from New York, on Long Island. My mother had called me that morning to say that he seemed extremely weak, maybe we'd better come. When we entered their apartment, she was sitting on the living-room sofa. Quiet. She gazed at me sorrowfully. "It's too late, Tobele. He died an hour ago."

And my husband's father. He, too, died in our absence. We were on a Caribbean island when the news came by phone. He had gone to work that morning, and while he was walking in the street his heart gave way and he sat down on a stoop and expired. That night we flew home. The plane was half empty as it vaulted through dark, cloudless space. The light of cities far below. It was a steady, quiet flight. My husband and I barely spoke. It is true what the Spaniards say: *Partir es morir un poco.* To depart is to die a little.

I never leveled with my father's prophecy, with his fear. Now I'm remorseful. I was trying to force him away from death, guilty of that common tacit assumption that thinking about death is willing oneself toward death, a defeated flight from the world. Public decorum —or is it security?—does not allow us the courage to admit anxiety about mortality. My father's thoughts were on death. He was foreseeing it, winding things up. He was ready. When did he start?

On the road from Seville to Jerez we see fields and fields of olive trees that have been uprooted in order to convert the field into a more lucrative yield, one that will meet the demands of a shifting world market. Gnarled trunks sprawl in upheaval. Dry branches clutch at the air, rooting round for the absent nipple of earth. It is a field strewn with corpses. An orchard in rigor mortis. The roots, black and charred, gape out of the hollows from which they were torn. Inert. Like teeth extracted from ragged gashes, blood-blackened, exposed to the merciless glare of Mediterranean sun. I, too, am uprooted from the soil from which I sprang. My vital sap drained. Inside is a hollow place that will never heal. A permanent wound.

"Go to Santiago de Compostela," our Sevillano friend, an architect, urges. *"Es formidable."* We make the pilgrimage. A plane to Madrid, then on to the northwest corner of Spain, to Galicia and the shrine of St. James. We stay at an old hostel in Santiago where weary medieval pilgrims once sought shelter at the end of the Holy Way. The hostel, subsequently a hospital where the infirm struggled against death, is now a splendid government parador which provides luxurious twentieth-century asylum to affluent tourists in cashmere and camel's-hair. A far cry from those past wayfarers who "took the cockleshell" and arrived in the pilgrims' uniform of heavy cape, eight-foot stave topped with water gourd, stout sandals, and broad-brimmed felt hats turned up in front and marked with three or four scallop shells.

We enter the carved Door of Glory of Santiago's Romanesque cathedral, built upon the original site of the first basilica, which in turn was erected over the apostle's tomb. Exhausted pilgrims, on entering, used to place their hands on the central pillar in token of safe arrival—a symbolic gesture which, repeated myriad times, left finger marks on the stone. We pass through the nave of the cathedral and stand before the majestic statue of St. James. Inside, friars and worshippers kneel and pray in deep devotion. Outside in the plazas, tourists circle the cathedral, which, unique in Spain, can be seen from plazas on all sides. University students sell postcards and records of regional dances.

We wander through the zigzagging cobbled streets of this misty medieval city with its stone buildings faced in fluted scallop shells. Students on holiday talk about Franco's demised regime, about democracy and the new Spain, about the right to strike, the Basque separatist movement, inflation, unemployment, Woody Allen, pornographic movies. In a noisy workers' café near the market, we drink white Ribeiro wine from creamy ceramic dishes that resemble rice bowls. In the marketplace, clear, blue-eyed peasant women, ruddy, big-bosomed, and dressed in black, are selling fresh Muenster cheeses. Ivory mounds, shaped like breasts, the color of mother's milk, and, in fact, called *tetas*, teats. The women are of that sturdy stock that reminds me of my mother's aunts: grocers' wives, tough ladies who lived in back of the store, nursed babies, stoked coal stoves, cooked, sold butter and cheese and pickles from the barrel.

These Galician women in the marketplace are superb. Bursting with vigor and energy, their skins coursing with blood, their ample bodies agile, their arms broad and firm, hands strong. Hands for doing. Hands that remind me of my mother's. As does their direct gaze. Four of them in a row selling their *teta* cheeses from baskets lined with leaves. When I try to snap their pictures, they laughingly raise their aprons to hide their faces. Then, as if on cue, and in unison, they turn and present their backsides to my poised camera. I hear their guffaws. My mother would have liked that. No monkey business, is the message. If you want to remember us, do so in your head. *That's* how you remember. In your head.

The numbers associated with her. 2009, Apartment 5G, that windblown house on the corner of Bronx Park East, the first house that I remember; 2045 Holland Avenue, Apartment 6C, where I lived from age five until I left their roof at age twenty for my first job outside the city; 321 West 90 Street, Apartment 7D, their last address. They didn't move around much. Westchester 7-4625, their first telephone number and mine. We were the first on our floor to get a phone, back in the thirties, and sometimes our neighbors would come in to use it. I still remember that number today, though it is some thirty years since last I dialed it. Trafalgar 7-8122, their final phone number. Who would answer if I dialed it now? Some strange voice, or would I get a busy signal, or is it dead? $133.70, the amount on the rent check I sent out for her each month. Who lives in Apartment 7D now, amid their footprints, fingerprints, smells, and echoes? Is there still the scent of fresh laundry?

They moved to 2045 Holland Avenue in order to be close to P.S. 105. The house and school were across a street with little traffic and I could go and return by myself.

In 1933, when you moved into an apartment building you were granted one month's concession—free rent—plus a fresh paint job, new linoleum, new window shades, and, if you pressed, even a new refrigerator or stove. My mother was very happy about the move. The new apartment was bright and sunny, with cross ventilation. There was a separate bedroom that my sister and I shared, plus a brand-new refrigerator *and* stove. The linoleum was an inlaid Armstrong, cream-colored, with a confetti pattern. In June, the house porter came around to attach striped awnings outside our windows. He did it every year. It was a sure sign of summer.

Apartment 6C was on the top floor. Climbing one flight of steps brought us out on the roof with its strings of clotheslines. Every Tuesday, washing day, my mother and I would climb up to the roof, she holding one handle of the wicker laundry basket, I the other, and while she stretched the clean wash on the line and fastened it with wooden clothespins to catch the sun and breezes, I was busy popping the tar bubbles that glistened in the sun and squishing the warm tar under my shoes. In late afternoon, we climbed up again to gather and fold the wash.

Milk was delivered at our front door every day, two bottles, pasteurized but not homogenized, laced with three inches of rich ivory cream on top. Twice a week the milkman brought a glass measure of heavy sweet cream, which we poured on baked apples, stewed prunes and apricots, chocolate pudding, and Jell-O. Once a week the soda man delivered a case of seltzer, turquoise bottles with metal noses and spouts, a half case of beer, both pilsner and light, which my father occasionally had with dinner. My sister and I would be given a sip.

Our old neighborhood, Pelham Parkway, was middle-class and fairly solid. The six-story houses, red or buff-colored brick, built mostly in the early thirties, often boasted a courtyard garden that fronted the main entrance. Spirea, forsythia, mountain laurel, juniper, and ivy bloomed in ours. The main entrance of our house was guarded by a uniformed doorman. The man on the night shift was also the sometime porter of the somber, musty lobby, dusting the dark, gloomy mission oak furniture and anointing it with lemon oil. He stored his dust cloths and polish in a heavily carved chest that swung open on creaky hinges. It looked like a coffin, and I always hurried past it on my way to the elevator, fearing that one of these days it might open spontaneously and a corpse would rise, maybe the ghost of

Mrs. Blotchinsky, that blue-haired elderly lady in Apartment 5G who had died of a heart attack and whose coffin was borne through that very lobby.

Our house was one of the few in the neighborhood that had its own playground, with swings, seesaw, a sandbox, benches for mothers where they could sit and knit or gossip, watching their children. It was fine when we were little, but as we grew older we preferred the wild stretches of the empty bordering lot. There on the scraggly, rocky slope we played tag, ring-a-levio, cops and robbers, hide-and-seek, freeze, and giant. There we found empty crates that served as kindling for fires to roast mickeys and marshmallows and to watch the melting colors of Bronx sunsets, there we chased butterflies and dissected weeds and flowers. Goldenrod, dandelion, Queen Anne's lace, milkweed, nettles, and thistles flourished amid flyaway newspapers and an occasional chunk of scrap iron. If you were lucky, you might also find an empty soda bottle that could be redeemed for two cents. At times, our wilderness was overrun by barbaric hordes of boys who wielded BB guns and practiced their aim by hitting bottles and cans—and us. At Halloween they whacked us with socks filled with chalk dust.

All the buildings in the neighborhood had alleys, wide air shafts which divided the sections of the building and provided back entrances into the dark, sweating basements. In those alley enclosures we played jacks, knucklebone, yo-yo, marbles, hi-li, statues, and take-a-giant-step. The older boys played handball against a wall and the girls played slug, a variation of handball for which you used a slightly larger, softer ball and allowed the ball to bounce in between plays: "A, my name is Annabel, and my husband's name is

Archibald, we come from Afghanistan, and we sell avocados." Sometimes we skipped rope and intoned, in screechy cronish voices:

> Last night and the night before
> A lemon and a pickle knocked at the door,
> I went downstairs to let them in,
> They hit me on the head with a bottle of gin.
> Lady, lady, turn around,
> Lady, lady, touch the ground.
> My mother says, out goes Y-O-U!

My friends and I also passed the time rubbing a peach pit on the ground till it took the shape of a ring, or we shaped balls out of rubber bands, or hooked endless tails on horse reins. Summer evenings, we caught fireflies in a jar and discussed the feasibility of digging and digging till we hit China. Time stretched on infinitely.

We played punchball, roller-skated, bicycled in the street. Came winter, we sampled the first snow on the tips of our tongues, built fat, effeminite snowmen, and went sleighing in the corner lot, where the pile of rubbish had been transformed into a beautiful snowy magic mountain.

What didn't we do? as my mother would say.

Our spots to play were chosen the way Spaniards buy tickets for the bullfight. There was *sol* and *sombra*, sun and shade. Winter mornings, we settled in the sunny courtyard, then later in the day followed the sun's rays like a leash to the benign warmth in front of the house. Our summer routine was exactly the opposite. Hot afternoons were idled away in the shady courtyard, where it was cool as a cave, and whose walls had been appropriately chalked with youthful cave drawings, our iconography, and whose cement floors bore the voodoo markings of hopscotch diagrams.

Our steadfast presence in the courtyard made us useful standbys for tenants in performing small services and favors. We kept an eye on babies napping in straw carriages and dogs on their leashes. Twice a day, Mrs. Bendel would hail us from her second-floor window and promptly lower a basket on a rope. Inside was Chan, her tiny white Pekinese, so well trained that the instant the basket touched ground he hopped out, scooted over to the hydrant, dispensed his pee-pee and "number two," promptly jumped back into the waiting basket, and crouched quietly while Mrs. Bendel hoisted him aloft.

Grownups never lingered in the courtyard. Their spot was at the front entrance, where, astride folding chairs, they scrutinized everyone entering and departing, exchanged gossip, recipes, hospital stories, and child-rearing advice. They eagerly availed themselves of our help: "Ask the soda man to leave me one dozen seltzer, a case of beer, six cream sodas, and six celery tonics." Or: "Tell the laundry man not to put so much starch in my husband's shirts, and tell him that I left our bundle of dirty wash in Apartment 3G." Or: "If my Aunt Sadie comes, tell her I went to Alexander's and the door is open and she should go in and make herself a nice glass of tea." Or: "Remind my husband when he comes home to put up the baked potatoes—I'm going to the chiropodist."

Whenever the merry-go-round came by, or the ambulatory ice-cream vendor in his yellow horse-drawn wagon, or Antonio, the mustachioed Sicilian who grated ices, or the old man who sold hot sweet potatoes and chestnuts, we'd rush beneath our windows to shout upstairs to our mothers for money. The coins showered down wrapped in tight wads of newspaper. When the barrel-organ grinder in bandanna and one earring came with his monkey, or the itinerant fiddler stood in the alley and launched into heartrending Hungarian melodies, they, too, were thrown coins enfolded in newsprint. Once a month came the scissors-grinder and knife sharpener, twice a month the ragman with rolled-up newspaper in hand and a burlap sack over his shoulder, singing, "I-cash-clothes . . . I-cash . . ." We trailed this Pied Piper down the block to tell him that Mrs. Reuben was on the lookout for him and was hailing him from her fourth-floor window.

The candy store was our local café. Run by Mr. and Mrs. Fine, a surly ma-and-pa team who reeked of salami and whose loathing for each other and impatience at our caprices bounced off the walls of their musty crowded store like slingshots. In those days, when kids were still called brats, we drove them crazy in our tormented indecision over two-for-a-penny or ten-for-a-penny items. Jelly beans were ten-for-a-penny; malted balls, two-for-a-penny. You also had the choice of root-beer barrels, chocolate babies, chicken-feed, chocolate-covered cherries, slices of halvah, long paper strips glued with multicolored sugary dots, three-cent or five-cent ice-cream cones with or without sprinkles, Popsicles, Fudgicles, three-cent egg creams, cherry sodas with a cherry at the bottom, thick sweet malteds to be eaten with a Hostess cupcake or a sticky Drake's cake, chocolate on the outside and a heart of sweet butter cream. We could also feed the nut machines, poppyseeds, pumpkin seeds, and Indian nuts, leaving trails of shells in our wake. Pity the unlucky kid who, after a bout of indecisiveness, marched out buying nothing. At the candy store, we exercised our first economic sanctions, boycotting during the second Sino-Japanese War those nickel and dime geegaws that bore the ignominious stamp: MADE IN JAPAN.

In winter, when flushed, we'd stroll to the bakery on the Avenue and, for five cents, splurge on a glistening ruby jelly apple or an ethereal charlotte russe. The Garden Bakery had the best charlotte russes; the Snowflake, across the street, the best jelly apples. Sometimes we bought a pomegranate and walked along eating it, spitting out the defoliated seeds—our breath was steamy, our noses runny, our mouths stained scarlet. Sundays, as a special treat, my friend and I sometimes went to the delicatessen for a corned-beef or pastrami sandwich on rye, dripping with yellow mustard and coleslaw.

Some days I went marketing with my mother. I walked along, hands hanging free. My sister often held my mother by her skirt or the fold of her coat. Our first stop was the butcher. Mr. Nussbaum, a *ganef*, but in his favor one had to admit that he carried "only the best." The sweetest, leanest, first-cut baby lamb chops, calves' liver from yesterday's slaughter, pullets sure to melt in your mouth. My mother, not given to bargaining, paid little attention to his insistence that for her the price was special. Mrs. Nussbaum, a phlegmatic woman in white apron, hair encased in a flowered kerchief, sat at the rear of the store plucking chicken feathers into the sawdust. Day in and day out, she observed her husband work, tossing slabs of liver, cuts of flanken, or a length of beef entrail onto the scale with the aplomb of a legerdemainist.

On the way to the vegetable market, we'd pass the

drugstore with its window emblazoned in an Ex-Lax emblem. Ex-Lax, Alphone pills, castor oil, milk of magnesia—laxatives in general—and enemas were the Valium of those days. Whatever bothered you, the front line of treatment was to clean out your stomach. Not the head, the nerves, the psyche—the stomach. In the window of the pharmacy, there were also two perennial apothecary jars, one filled with red liquid, the other with blue; there was a mortar and pestle, vessels of medicinal herbs, a plaster cast of fallen arches, a dummy wearing a truss for that unmentionable problem—hernia—from which my Uncle Jack suffered. At the drugstore we used to buy those two-inch squares of camphor ice which my sister and I, along with all the other children in the neighborhood, strung round our necks during polio season—late spring and summer—to ward off the dread disease. It was also where you bought calamine lotion for poison ivy, Dr. Stokes' Expectorant for bronchial cough, red enema bags, tar shampoo for lice, cod-liver oil for winter salubrity. Medicines were less sophisticated than nowadays, and in our house especially, colds tended to be confronted with a good dose of fresh onion.

Farther down the avenue was Oxman's, a family dry-goods store that sold everything from snowsuits and jock straps and plaid flannel bathrobes to towels and rubber sheets for bed wetters; Horowitz's grocery store, the "appetizer," the Chinese laundry, the "new" bakery —a mere ten years old—where for a dime you could buy a pound loaf of rye bread with either poppy or caraway seeds and so well baked it crackled when you squeezed it, and on Friday, Sabbath eve, a twisted hallah, glossy brown on the outside, egg yellow on the inside.

Certain seasonal tasks were family events. Autumn, we made wine from Concord grapes. The grapes came in wooden boxes that held five pounds. Usually we bought three of those boxes. My sister and I sampled so many of the tart grapes that our lips prickled and our mouths and teeth were stained deep purple. Enough is enough, said my mother, but enough was never enough. As the grapes were being washed by my father, you could reel from their heady, winy odor. My mother placed the washed grapes into large crockery vats and covered them with cheesecloth so that they could breathe. A few months later, the wine would be siphoned from the vats, the skins pressed, and the purple juice transferred into fresh vats, which were stored in the foyer closet. That dark closet was our wine cellar; it also held our potatoes. It was the place once in the middle of the night where my mother found me sleep-walking. "What are you doing here?" she asked. "I came to get a potato," I told her.

Every few years my mother refilled our goose-down pillows. She'd sit on the rim of the bathtub, my sister and I nearby, and rip open the end seam of the pillows, emptying the feathers into the tub. While my sister and I held the new ticking, she'd pour in the old feathers plus plenty of fresh ones. Kerchiefs were tied low on our foreheads, but the feathers invariably flecked our lashes and eyebrows and crept into our nostrils. I'd sneeze, my mother laughed. Little feathers clung to the strands of raven-black hair peeking from her kerchief. They looked like flakes of snow. Once, while she was elbow deep in feathers, her wedding band accidentally fell off. Oh, how worried she was. The three of us began rummaging around frantically in the tub. I was the one who jubilantly fished it out. If I remember, that occasion prompted her to award me one of her medals.

On Saturday nights, if my parents went out, they left my sister and me in the care of Lily, the daughter of our once-a-week cleaning woman. A lively black girl of seventeen, she applied various intriguing ointments and balms to her face and hair and slept in a stocking cap. She'd giggle an awful lot and tell us chilling stories about bats and ghosts till we were so scared we hid under the covers, where those winged mice could not entangle themselves in our hair and ghosts might overlook us. We loved it when Lily came. She always slept over, since my parents' outings at the card table wound up at unpredictable hours. Once in a while, my paternal grandfather stopped by, like a figure in one of our pop-up picture books—the bell rang and there he was. There was *zayde*, the grandfather. All the way from Middle Village, borough of Queens. Fiery eyes, bristly beard, tufts of hair sprouting from his nostrils, black hat, black gaberdine suit and vest. He gave my sister and me a cursory look—to this day, I'm not certain he knew our names; there was something terribly absent about the man—sometimes he shoved a bag of rock candy into our hands, then headed straight for the kitchen to ransack the refrigerator. He'd picnic for a long time and finally emerge smelling of herring, beard flecked with silvery fish scales, egg yolk, or borscht.

My mother used to complain about the mess he left, but never scolded the old man. When he was hospitalized during his final illness and wouldn't eat the hospital food, fearing, despite reassurances, that it was unkosher, she'd bring him jars of soup, boiled chicken, and applesauce.

Bronx Park was my wilderness. My friends and I loved to wander in the woods. We padded over the run-

ners of moss that climbed round the roots and base of
trees. We gathered fern and dogwood and wild sumac.
Scaled hills, where we pictured feathered Indians once
roaming in savage bliss. We surprised beaver and rac-
coon and porcupine scuttering in the underbrush. In
spring, we trekked over the thawing ground, lush with
clumps of skunk cabbage and jack-in-the-pulpit, inhaling the deep organic pungency of marsh, loam, and
growth. We gathered bouquets of spring beauties, anem-
one, violets, and wild calla. Picked sticky, swelling pop-
lar buds, pointed like candle tapers that had been ignited
by the sun. Plucked stubby buds off the maples, little
orange and red rosettes of flame. We'd lie in a field of
new clover grass, turning our faces to air soft as buttercup
blossoms, promising as the green blades jutting forth
from earth. The sweet presence of spring made me want
to whoop like a fool and dance till entwined in the may-
pole of the wind, weightless as those darting ribbons of
golden light.

In fall, our house was invaded by the sheaves of
tawny oak leaves, which I carted home by the armful,
and the fallen acorns, which I'd connect with tooth-
picks to make dollhouse furniture. The acorns, after a
month or so, began crawling with worms, to my sister's
shrieks of disgust, and my mother's admonition to get
rid of the "livestock." I collected specimens of all the
autumn leaves—birch and beech and sycamore—and
arranged and labeled them in my botanical scrapbook.
I looked up the Latin names of the flowers, identified
the species, dreamed of going to the Alps to find specimens of blue gentian and green-flowered asphodel.

As I grew older and strayed farther from 2045, I had
the habit of walking to the IRT subway station at
Bronx Park East to await my father's return from work.

I'd stand under the massive El structure watching for that first glimpse of him. He was usually on a train that arrived shortly before five. I was always early. The East 241 Street locals and expresses roared deafeningly overhead. Tracks and platform rumbled. It was always dark and isolated under the tracks, with spooky shadows cast by those great supporting columns. The place had a special gritty smell. When you stood on the platform waiting for a train, you could see the wheels shooting blue-white sparks against the black tracks like the sparklers given to children as a bonus when they bought a new pair of shoes from the neighborhood Stride-Rite shoe store. But beneath the platform it was eternally dark, the sun never penetrating.

I felt lonely there, in that hollow space with its dead odor, and was relieved when at last I spotted my father at the top of the long stairway. Excited, I moved forward. His tired face lit up as our eyes met. He descended the fifty-two steps. We embraced. He kissed me, one of those gargantuan kisses which wet my cheek, much to my distaste. His face was stubbly. A hairy man by nature, he had sprouted beard amply between dawn, when he set out for work, and dusk, when he returned. From the gnarled Italian woman in black who sold newspapers, gum, candy, and cigarettes at the little stand by the station, he bought the late edition of *The New York Sun*, which published the closing stock-market quotations, and a Hershey bar for me. He held my hand as we walked home. I felt his physical strength. I remember his smell of sweat, work, the outdoors, and the smell of fresh newsprint. As he returned from work, his pace was slower and I didn't have to hurry to keep up with him as I did when he was fresh. My father was a walker. As I am now. A fast walker, he

was. As I am now. And in those days I tried to walk as
straight and sturdy as he. When we reached home, my
mother had dinner waiting.

On Sundays, when we were very young, my father
would take my sister and me for a long walk in Bronx
Park. Often, he'd pick up a freshly fallen branch from
the path and peel the bark with his key into totem-pole
designs, alternate bands of stripes and crosses. My sister and I, as we skipped along, would tap the shadows
and ruts of the dappled path with our new sticks. Usually we carried some bread crumbs to feed the purple-
and green-feathered ducks that paddled in the Bronx
River. Sometimes we went as far as the zoo, where we
saw peacocks, pheasants, enormous grouse with feath-
erless necks and wrinkled, knobby faces. There were
crocodiles and hippopotamuses and bears and kan-
garoos and sloths and seals and zebra and armadillos
and auks and newts and ibex and oryx and platypuses.
By the time I reached ten, I knew every path and animal house in the Bronx Zoo—though I'd never yet
been to Manhattan. Nowadays, when I visit the Central
Park Zoo, a miniature alongside that other vast park, I
recall those happy days when I'd be dashing along the
path ahead of my father, swinging a walking stick that
he'd made for me. Those happy days when I had total
faith. And was untouched by doubt.

My sister's favorites were the monkeys, and we'd
stand in front of their cages for the longest time, gawk-
ing at them as they swung on the bars, exhibited their
whorled assholes, preened each other assiduously, and
made faces at the public. My father would invent one
of his silly ditties: "All the monkeys in the zoo, they
will say hello to you." Sometimes we rented a rowboat,
and while my sister and I leaned back or glided our

hands in the water, my father rowed. I listened to the sound of the oars, the backwash of water like a deep sigh, and I watched those powerful hairy arms propel the boat across the river and knew that my father's strength could protect me from anything.

We came home at around four to early Sunday dinner. A big pot of thick pea soup crowded with boiled beef, marrow and knuckle bones, or a mushroom and barley soup with both fresh and dried mushrooms, or maybe borscht or stuffed cabbage. My mother would have washed her hair and it gleamed like black satin. After we'd eaten, my parents would stretch out to rest on their bed and talk in restful tones while my sister and I played rowdily at fiddlesticks, anagrams, bingo, or Monopoly, or hid under the patterned summer slipcover which bloomed on the dining table, our secret garden of vines and trellises and birds where we took stock of the world, or we might even cook up some pasty concoction on our toy electric stove, the base of the dish usually oatmeal or Ralston.

In the evening an aunt or uncle might visit. My aunts, whose kindly breasts spread in all directions, and their husbands with vests and watch fobs. They came bearing a beribboned box of chocolates, Schrafft's or Barricini, or some glazed fruits—you never visited empty-handed. My sister and I saved the boxes. The grownups sat around our dining-room table and cracked walnuts and almonds, drank tea, ate apples that were pared in one long dangling strip, red on one side, white on the other. My mother had a trick I admired enormously—without use of a knife, she could twist an apple clear in half.

On alternate Sundays we'd make the interminable voyage to visit my grandparents, who lived in a row house in Middle Village. I was always struck by that evocative name, and wondered where it was in the middle of? America? The world? Anyhow, that trip necessitated three subway changes, plus a bumpy trolley ride over the odoriferous Canarsie River, and finally an ancient bus. My father carried my sister, and the polish on her white shoes invariably smudged his navy-blue suit, both she and I invariably got carsick, and all of us were invariably cranky and exhausted by the time we made the return trek on Sunday night. Those Sundays were of a piece. Afternoon dinner with my grandparents. Grandfather, a feisty, bearded patriarch; grandmother a gentle, sickly woman with chronic ailments such as diabetes, high blood pressure, and heart disease; my father's five sisters, two unmarried and firmly anchored at home, the other three dwelling in dutiful proximity with their respective mates in Middle Village. My father would often fall asleep after dinner. After about five years of these bimonthly filial visits, my mother put her foot down and asked my father to make the pilgrimage alone.

On summer evenings, supper was over by half past six. It was still daylight, and my father rested over his newspaper, listening to Elmer Davis, William Shirer, and Amos 'n Andy. My mother would be cleaning up in the kitchen. My friends and I played in the street. In the distance we could hear the clanging streetcars rattling along their tracks, and through the open windows came the sound of radios. This was the background to our skip-rope chants, or knock-knock jokes, and when we were older, to the current songs we sang from the Saturday Night Hit Parade. *Pardon me, boy, is this the Chattanooga choo-choo?* Or: *I'm gonna buy a paper*

doll that I can call my own . . . For ten cents, we used
to buy a printed, colored sheet with all the words.
Sometimes one of us brought down a bag of hard June
peaches or a pound of sour cherries and we'd gorge.
When it grew dark and the blue pincushion sky became
studded with quivering stars, my mother's voice called
out from our sixth-floor window, "Come home. Make
night."

I grew up in a neighborhood steeped in permanence.
A world that was warm and confined and promised to
go on forever. But in the background a man named
Hitler was fast becoming the ruler of Germany. His
voice sputtered over the radio. Poland was invaded.
Europe was being overrun by the Nazis. Churchill
gravely accepted the challenge. War. My friends and I
went to the Red Cross after school to fold bandages.
We saved nylon stockings for parachutes and clipped
ration stamps. We knitted and knitted, for "the boys."
I'd hear my mother talking to my father about *haim*,
home. Nervously, they'd turn the radio knobs for news-
casts. There was talk of refugees. There were air-raid
drills. English broadcasts began with the first four
notes of Beethoven's Fifth Symphony. My mother had
stopped sending those packages of food and clothing
which my father through the years had toted to the
post office. She no longer knew where to send them.
Mail from her family had broken off. Never did she
receive specific news of her father's death, she never
knew exactly when he and her brothers and sisters and
grandmother perished. Death happened behind her
back. She cried. Now both mother and father were
dead, ravaged by European history, wars, pestilence,
extermination camps. A few more invisible people gone.

Another family tree burnt nearly to a stump. I was too young to understand what such horror, violence, and repressed grief meant in her life.

Once I also saw my father cry. It was the day they called from Montefiore Hospital to tell him that his father had died. Cancer. My father looked stunned when he heard the news. I knew it was something bad. He went to his bedroom and threw himself face down on the bed. And wept. For a year he went twice a day to say Kaddish. A son, they say, is his father's future Kaddish. Sometimes I'd go with him to the evening service. It was in a little wooden storefront synagogue on the Avenue, flanked on one side by Malkin's Yarns and on the other by Shapiro's kosher butcher. I remember those wooden benches, the stale air of snuff, the elders in their white and blue silk prayer shawls, the old dog-eared books with the black Hebrew hieroglyphics. I remember being surrounded by men in yarmulkes, or black hats, swaying back and forth, moving to the earth's sway, chanting in singsong voices what was to become for me the familiar Hebrew words of the Kaddish.

An undated memory: I learn that death can happen to anyone. Before your eyes, as instantaneous as when you step on an ant and it ceases to move.

It was after school, on one of those days in early spring. As I came through the courtyard, my little sister was playing with her friends. "Ashes, ashes, all fall down!" The circle of children collapsed like a ring of marionettes whose string has gone slack. My sister broke from the circle as I came out of the doorway.

"Where are you going? Take me with you!"

She always wanted to trail me everywhere. Normally

I'd have agreed, but today, with the first whiff of spring, I needed to go alone. I felt like a kite that had to fly off unattached for a reunion with the sun.

All traces of winter were going, going, gone. Itchy woolen ski pants that chaffed your thighs, sleds, ice skates. The new season was on the block. Soft air panted like a puppy round my bare arms and legs and tousled my loose hair. Upstairs, my mother was arranging ruffles of fresh organdy curtains on a newly washed kitchen window. Downstairs, kids on the block had fished out their roller skates from the closet and were gliding down the hill, their skate keys bouncing on the string round their necks. Others were playing jacks on the stoop. Boys in knickers were thumping a handball against the brick wall.

By now, I had known enough springtimes to have expectations. I was able to predict the season's course, sense the renewal of life. I was aware, young, and immortal.

"Take me with you!" my sister begged.

"Not today. I'm crossing the street." She wasn't allowed to cross the street.

First she pouted in disappointment, but then shrugged and wedged her way back into the circle.

"Tomorrow," I promised, calling over my shoulder.

I crossed the small street separating my block from P.S. 105. It was the street I crossed every morning, the street I'd been crossing for three years since I began school, a single safe crossing which enabled me to come and go on my own.

Walking past the school's front entrance, I turned the corner toward the western façade, heading toward the entrance of the schoolyard and Play Street. Today was the first day of the marble season. Till now it had been too cold, and then the ground too muddy. A little leather pouch filled with old marbles—my favorite lucky green, and some shiny, unscratched new ones—dangled from my hand.

Play Street was bustling. All the neighborhood kids were out. The street was noisier than usual. In the lot facing Play Street, a new building was under construction. Rumor was that it would be the most modern in the neighborhood—dropped living rooms, air conditioning—and incoming tenants would be lured not only with the usual premium stove, refrigerator, and linoleum, but with two months' rent concession, plus—modernity of modernities—venetian blinds.

In the empty lot where the building was to rise, I saw a bulldozer charging across the lot like a snorting dragon, leaving in its wake a gaping hole for the foundation. A construction crane with enormous spindly arms was swallowing tons of dirt in its rusted ancient jaw. Workers scurried back and forth shouting commands to one another. The air smelled raw, of unearthed dirt, dampness, construction sand.

My friends were waiting for me. Plump Roslyn, whiny red-haired Muriel, white-skinned Bernice, whose eyes were the color of my clearest blue marble, clever Eleanor, a whiz in arithmetic and with penmanship so perfect it looked machine-made. The five of us had been in the same class since kindergarten. For three years we'd lined up in size-place, helped each other with homework, confessed our angers and fears, passed messages in class, pulled each other's hair in skirmish, made modest exhibitions of sex, administered first aid to scraped knees, licked each other's ice cream cone and sprinkles, caught each other's measles and whooping cough.

"Where's Rozzie?" Eleanor asked straightaway. My friends were so used to seeing her with me, they thought of us as attached, like paper dolls.

"She's listening to the radio," I lied.

We walked past a group of boys playing Johnny-on-a-pony against the wire grating of the schoolyard, searching for a spot for our game of marbles. A place to set down the empty cigar box that Muriel had brought to serve as Home. The goal of the game was to roll the marbles from a distance toward the open box and see who could get the most up its slope and into the empty box.

"How's this?" Bernice asked above the roar of the bulldozer.

"What?" Muriel shouted.

"How about playing here?" Bernice asked.

The normal calm of our untrafficked Play Street was disrupted by the activity in the building lot. But we did not consider moving elsewhere. This was our territory.

We set the box in position, drew a chalk line to mark the starting spot, and spent a few moments admiring each other's new marbles: the ruby-red purees, the fat-striped marbles that looked like Christmas candy, the clear green and blue ones that were like sandglass, liquid-seeming as life itself. I turned one about till it shone with a ray of gold. Then, quickly, we abandoned ourselves to the game. As absorbed as poker players. For, depending on luck, skill, and concentration, you could return home with leather pouch doubled or near empty. So engrossed were we that the roar of the bull-dozer and of incoming trucks delivering construction sand and towing away rubble soon became mere rumbles in the background.

Amid one of her plays, Bernice's prize agate marble,

a fat opaque purple-and-yellow-striped sphere, the one she used for bumping opponents, rolled off the sand of our territory and into the street. It whirled across the asphalt. Still in crouched position, Bernice hopped off like a rabbit to rescue it.

The rest of us, huddled around the cigar box, spied a construction truck, its back raised from having dumped a load, back up out of the lot. The driver, his view blocked, moved steadily backward. Bernice, intent only on catching her runaway marble, never even noticed the moving vehicle. In a split second, before we knew it and before we could move, she was under its wheels. She uttered no sound, no brakes screeched. We screamed.

It was too late. When the truck moved forward again, Bernice remained behind, flat on the ground. Her head was crushed, her chin jutted up. One foot was bare and thrust outward in ballet position. Her arm, outstretched, was reaching still for the marble.

We stood numb. Across the way, we saw workers hurrying to the fallen girl. They felt her pulse, listened to her heart, placed a mirror in front of her mouth, then covered her with a canvas drop cloth. Minutes later, a police siren shrieked into Play Street. I heard a policeman say, "Who knows her parents?"

We went over. I spoke.

"Her name is Bernice Cohen. Her family lives at 2047 Holland Avenue. Yes, right opposite the school."

I looked at Bernice's straw-blond hair. It was matted with dark red blood that reminded me of the blood splattered on the white feathers of the pullets Mrs. Nussbaum plucked at the butcher's.

All the way home, I tried to imagine Mrs. Cohen's face when the police brought her the news. And Mr.

Cohen, when he returned home from work, as on every other day, how soon would he be learning that all days are not alike.

One day does not invariably follow like every other, seasons do not always bring predictable changes, I would not have Bernice for a friend any more. The world was small and terrible.

I reached my house. My sister and her friends were still circling in their game, chanting: "Ring around a rosy, pockets full o' posies, ashes, ashes, all fall down!"

And then there was school. Public school 105. A six-story no-nonsense brick building with a wire-enclosed schoolyard where inmates lined up each morning in size-place to wait for the gong and file in. Gray stone stairways, Up and Down, and God forbid you should reverse the direction; Lysol-smelling toilets, the Boys' of particular interest for those mysterious elongated white-enamel basins; water fountains in yawning corridors where a lukewarm trickle gurgled in desertlike dearth; classrooms with oak desks screwed immutably to the floor, their wooden surfaces interrupted at the upper right-hand corner by a circular enclosure and inkwell; the American flag presiding over the front blackboard, and the black horizontal streamer bordering the top inscribed with the white letters of the alphabet, in upper and lower case.

Every morning you pledged allegiance to the flag, unpacked your books, arranged your pencils in the horizontal groove at the top of your desk, and took out your notebook. Those ten-cent notebooks, with their stiff covers in black and tawny water-wave design and off-gray cloth bindings.

Every day there was morning inspection of your person. You stood at attention alongside your desk while the teacher came around with her chart attached to a clipboard. Various numbers were accorded to various improprieties: #1–dirty nails, #2–dirty ears, #3–dirty neck, #4–dirty shoes, #5–lack of handkerchief—which was either prominently pinned to your dress or stuck under your Mickey Mouse watch. No one ever used that clean handkerchief. There was also a #6, but I forget what that was for.

The little inkwell at the corner of the desk was my *bête noire*. Penetrating its mysteries was prohibited until third grade, at which time we were considered "ready" to wield a pen and begin exercising our fingers with horizontal interlocking wave curves. This was a prelude to scrawling cramped, cursive letters with scratchy steel nibs inserted in wooden penholders. I was notably slow in catching on to the secrets of stiletto and ink, splattering my hands, the paper, and often my starched dress or middy in my bungling exertions. In my adulthood, when I switched from writing the letter S in cursive style to script, I did so with an enormous liberation, also with a certain trepidation, as if that third-year teacher, Mrs. Glite, was glaring reprovingly over my shoulder at this heresy of mine.

All day we sat at our desks, hands folded, back erect, eyes glued on the progress of the pointer, a tapered stick wielded by the teacher which pointed now at the blackboard, now at a pupil, now at a wrathful God. When called upon, we promptly sprang to our feet to the left of our seat, spoke up in a clear voice, waited for the signal of approbation or disgrace, then for the cue to be seated. Merciful teachers allowed their students to move around the room every couple of hours in order to release their charged-up restlessness. In midmorning there was a twenty-minute recess, during which the girls jumped double-Dutch in the yard and the boys tussled in touch football.

On Wednesday mornings there was Assembly. The girls wore navy-blue pleated skirts, a starched white middy, and a long green tie. I think we wore green because both the principal and the assistant principal were Irish. If, God forbid, a pupil wasn't properly attired for the occasion, he or she was quarantined in Room 107 with other delinquents.

On Friday mornings, tests. Penmanship tests, arithmetic tests, spelling tests. Writing neatly was as important as regurgitating the right answers. Friday afternoons, we had spelling bees. My sister used to vomit every Friday morning before going to school.

If late for school, you were detained after school. You had to sit still, with hands folded, for an unbearably long time, or you might have to write one hundred times, neatly, *I must not be tardy.* I would sit with my hands folded so hard, the intertwined fingers turned white. By the time release from detention came, I could fly into a frenzied dervish dance. After three latenesses, your mother was summoned by the teacher for an explanation. Faulty alarm clocks and lost shoes were unacceptable excuses. Should the lack of punctuality persist, Mother was called to the assistant principal's office.

I was in the top academic rung of the class and generally received an A in work, though often a C in conduct. Teachers claimed that I talked out of turn, whispered to my classmates. Fortunately, they were unaware of my other misdemeanors—that while my furrowed brow seemingly cogitated upon the multiplication table, carrying 3, actually I was daydreaming out the window; that while reading about Dick and Jane, I was painstakingly drawing naked bodies modeled after those I'd seen in the *Book of Knowledge*, volume 14, page 1173, under the entry for Michelangelo; that while seated in assembly listening to Mr. Ullman's peroration on Arbor Day, I was staring at the clocks on his socks and wondering what would happen if he unzipped his fly.

Our report cards in time became more refined. Bowing to updated pedagogical sophistication, they were divided into Work and Character. Character was further subdivided into Effort, Consideration for Others, etc. Your parents had to sign your report card after each "period." There were three periods to the term. My father used to sign mine. He was proud of my academic achievement, perplexed about the character evaluation. He knew I was a good girl. My mother was pleased with my A's, though untroubled by lesser grades, and completely unmindful of what the teachers had to say about my character.

Most of the children in P.S. 105 were Jewish. There were only two Italian families and one black poor family from the outskirts of our neighborhood. Classes were organized on the track system, according to academic ability. There were four classes in each grade. The "1" class was the brightest, the "3," not quite as bright, the "2" further down, and the "4," the dumbest. Your intelligence or lack of it was public knowledge. Promotion wasn't automatic. It was possible to be left back. It was also possible to be summoned to the front of the room and exiled to a blackboard corner, or, even worse, for an inquisitorial teacher to grasp your shoulders and shake you publicly to exorcise your wickedness and humiliate you at large, thus providing an example to other potential malefactors. It happened to me one Monday morning. As Mrs. Lozito was shaking me, I retasted the cod-liver oil my mother had given me that morning with my orange juice. I never told my parents about it. I didn't want to aggravate my mother, and I was ashamed to tell my father. How could he accept this affront upon his "golden child"?

These days I often forget the names of next-door neighbors, of people met at dinner parties, names that tease the tip of my tongue. But how can I ever forget the name of Mrs. Lozito, whose eyes popped as she shook me? Or of Mrs. Lavender, who burst out crying when an irate school-bus driver left us stranded on an excursion to Bear Mountain? Or of Mr. Ullman and Mr. Gimpelson, the only male teachers in P.S. 105? Or of Mrs. Feeney, who taught me the cross-stitch? I'll never forget any of them.

Home and school were apart. There was a clear demarcation in my life between the decorum of the classroom and the reality of home and of neighborhood streets. I wanted to be "good" in school, but felt that the rules would always trip me up. Stand up straight. Stop squirming. Cover your mouth when you cough. Turn your face away when you sneeze. Don't whisper. Don't daydream. Don't put your hand there. Endless mandates. The teachers were sentries rather than charmers. Only on Friday afternoons, when they read aloud from Kipling, *Johnny Kelly*, or *Alice in Wonderland*, did I suspect that school might have something to do with the pleasure stemming from words.

My own perception of how vast was the world of letters came when I joined the local public library. The Van Nest branch was about half a mile from my house, outside our neighborhood. You had to walk through a shadowy solitary section under the elevated and then into the Italian neighborhood. It had the aspect of an illicit expedition. Circumstances forced me to join the library under an assumed given name: the librarian refused to believe that Toby was not a nickname. On the spot I invented Yvette, which suited her fine, and for years my library card bore that pseudonym: Yvette Tolpen. The long walk to the library was a special pilgrimage. I went loaded with six books—the maximum you could borrow—and returned with another six. At home, I lost myself in reading. Read at every opportunity, at the dinner table, in bed after the lights were supposed to be out, and when I was sick. That was one of the dividends in being sick. Words and paragraphs and pages were lush private forests that you could invade and inhabit, where you detached yourself from other people and found clues to yourself. I owned few books, our house was not encased in shelves. I owned the library, and the librarian was my majordomo.

For my twelfth birthday, my parents bought a set of the *Book of Knowledge* from a door-to-door salesman from the Grolier Society. It was bound in maroon leather, had glossy vellum paper, and smelled of ink. The text was illustrated with engravings and colored pictures. I pored through the twenty volumes, consuming first the stories and legends, then the "Book of Golden Deeds" (profiles on heroes, explorers, prophets, and saints), then the "Book of Wonder," which answered such basic questions as: Why do I laugh and cry? Could we walk without toes? Why is it dark at night? Does a fish feel? Does the air ever get used up? Then I went on to the "Book of Familiar Things," which described The

Talking Machine (phonographs), The Ship Beneath
the Water (submarines), and Ships That Sail the Sky.
Secretly, I ogled the naked pictures in the World of Art,
studying my own future anatomical potential and certain curious male appendages. In an exquisite trance, I
pored over photographs of the Alps, Cambodia, Machu
Picchu. The pages of that encyclopedia are today dog-
eared and smudged with jam, the poetry section especially. I never underlined a single sentence. The encyclopedia was sacrosanct. For my fourteenth birthday, my
parents presented me with a mahogany secretary desk.
To study.

I hear my father, I need never fear. I hear my
mother, I'll not be lonely or want for love. As a child,
falling asleep amid the shifting shadows and shafts of
light, beneath those familiar cracks on my ceiling, I
could hear my parents' voices from their bedroom. I'd
hear that peaceful murmur, for a child the most lulling
bedtime sound in the world. My sister snored in the
bed next to mine. Our house heaved and breathed
gently. I listened to the spaces and heard the darkness
flowing from room to room. The walls held our home in
snug embrace, separating it from the windblown roof
and chimneys, the streets and street lamps, the flyaway
newspapers, the outside world. Homesick was a word I
didn't know. I could always return to my sixth floor.

June. Again. Ordinary tasks loom as obstacles.
The everyday business: planning dinner, answering the
telephone, attending film screenings. I am an idle onlooker dragged from her chair. Robotlike, I teach my

classes. The names of students, memorized the second week into the semester, have slipped from my mind. The fine shades of language, the delightful nuances of the subjunctive fail to provide their subtle pleasures. The "toward-which" and the "in-order-to," the way the present is rooted in the future and in having been, are phenomena which no longer titillate my mind. Like a dog baying at the moon, I transmit new conjugations. *Vivir*: to live; a regular *ir* verb, third conjugation. *Morir*: to die; an irregular verb of the same conjugation. *Ser*: to be. *Estar*: to be. *Ser*: to be, permanent; *estar*: to be, transient. Spanish, I point out, is the only Romance language which has two verbs for existence. *"El único ser es estar"*: the only true being is temporal —Unamuno. How many times have I cited this quote as mere grammatical allusion? Why did its meaning never penetrate?

Students come after class to negotiate grades, explain absences, deliver excuses, offer makeups, present papers, seek linguistic explanations, advice on career, life plans, corroboration. I adjust their records, explicate, nod. I bite my lips so as not to blurt out my pessimistic judgment of the noun *life*.

Youthful faces cram the elevators, the cafeterias. They sit before me in the classroom, in bluejeans, boots, bright-colored sweaters, earrings, plaid shirts, watches. They nod, smile, flirt, giggle, eat snacks, and drink Cokes. They hustle. They study.

My chalk scrawls verbs, diagrams, quotations, bibliographies on the blackboard. References scutter across slate. Chalk squeaks. The students shiver. Chalk dust powders my fingers. My mouth and nose go dry as dust.

Final exams get composed, Xeroxed, proctored,

graded. Everything happens. I go through the acts in the present *as if* I'm present. I behave *as if* it all mattered. Posturing in the imperfect subjunctive.

Outside Fordham University, I pass a Chaim Gross sculpture, Mother Playing. I stand crying in the homeless wind.

Suddenly I notice that in the streets people are dressed in summer clothes. Eating ice-cream cones. Wearing sunglasses. It's June. The seasons are happening. "Time to install the air conditioner," my husband remarks. Which means the handyman must be called. One more effort, one more hurdle. Winter garments need to be cleaned, camphored, transferred to make room for summer cottons, tennis whites, bathing suits.

On my way to the subway, approaching the bustling intersection of Eighty-sixth Street and Broadway, I spot, at a distance, Francisco. In gray suit and felt hat. Posted in the middle of the sidewalk, a foot or two in front of the corner building. With hands clasped over his belly, head tilted to the sun, he stands still as a scarecrow, a benign smile alight on his face. Totally impervious to the comings and goings of the crowd. Attentive only to the warm rays of the new season.

June.

My mother is dead.

Mourning has made me self-absorbed, unconcerned about the most momentous world events. The world is busy. Pakistan has been swallowed in a mouthful. Cuba is sending troops to Angola. Unemployment is rising, or is it dropping?

My so-called sunny nature has changed overnight. It

projects failure on every enterprise, universal emptiness. I see only futility. For the first time, I can't put on the old stiff upper lip. "Wipe that smile off your face," said Mrs. Lozito, my fifth-grade teacher. Well, I have. Left to my true desire, I'd sit in the dark and stare in stony silence. Among certain primitive tribes, the bereaved traditionally lops off the upper joint of her forefinger. At least that gives the mourner something to do, something to show for her misery. I do not care to cook meals, or go through other wifely and motherly motions. I do not care, as I once did, to feed the world. To respond with encouragement. To love. In mourning, no love is left for anyone.

I must not, I tell myself, hurt my family. Impose my suffering. Depression is contagious. With a bad headache, any bad hurt, it's best to go into your room and shut the door till the hurt goes away. Excessive mourning is nonproductive, someone remarks. A social inconvenience, downright inconsiderate in the public eye. Life, according to my Orientalist friend, is a passage, a corridor, and she bids me to rid myself of morbid brooding.

Bullshit! I'm angry. It's all a rotten hoax, this life of ours. You go from zero to zero. Why attach yourself to love only to have your beloved ripped from you? The upshot of love is pain. Life is a death sentence. Better not to give yourself to anything. The more you give, the more is taken from you. It's like stitching away only to discover at the end of the seam that you had no knot at the other end of the thread.

"Let death be thy teacher," said St. Augustine. Death *is* my teacher. Care less, be less vulnerable, for in the end, it all boils down to the same thing. The aim of life is death. Hence, let all of life mean less.

The healing professions have their one-word prescription for the consolation of grief. Empathy. But in moments of greatest pain no one can do a thing for anyone else. Death for the survivor is pain and hurt. It is loss and crying and living without. At times I think to myself: She wouldn't have wanted to bequeath a legacy of disintegration. I can see her tossing me one of her shrewd looks and saying, "Come on, snap out of it!"

Even now, as I think of her, that familiar swelling constricts my throat, turns it into a lump of clay, which means I can cry. But in the throes of tears, memories inevitably get foreshortened. Reduced to freeze shots of her in the hospital, in the coffin. Then again, silently, incredulously, I have to begin from the beginning and repeat: She's dead. As if it's just struck me. And I find myself drowning, engulfed by the disorder of the current, wanting to seize her hand to bring me to shore. Missing her so. Futilely trying to recapture that profile of elusive contours and shapes. To crystallize that deceased being. To evoke that palpable presence, the voice, inflections, and rhythms, the silences, expressions, gestures, stance, gait, the birthmarks and quirks. But the subject, prey like a shadow figure to shifting forms and arbitrary juxtapositions, omissions and simplifications, becomes indistinct.

And then the idealization. Another distortion. Idealizing her in a way antithetical to her nature. Bella was no lofty madonna, no enigmatic Mary, no *mater dolorosa*. She was a flesh-and-blood lady who got her hands wet, whose life encompassed pain and suffering. A human being with human flaws. It's a betrayal to remember only the good parts. Devoid of exertion, or resistance, or failure.

I remember that apartment where I grew up. I dream about it still. 6C. 2045 Holland Avenue. There were three and a half rooms: a kitchen, a dining room, a large foyer that served as sitting room, my parents' bedroom, and the room my sister and I shared, the "half room" off the kitchen, separated from it by an archway. In my parents' bedroom stood a bedstead of beech wood with matching bureau, dresser, and vanity. On the top of the vanity lay a tortoise vanity set, a wedding gift I believe, which included brush, comb, nail buffer, and mirror. On rainy days my sister and I used to play with them. My parents' wedding picture hung over their bed. My father looked young and tall and solemn. My mother wore a white veil low on her forehead and billowing round her face. In the kitchen was a white enamel table chipped on the left-hand corner, three chairs, a high chair, ruffled organdy curtains on the window. The window faced the courtyard.

I remember one day. It was dawn. I was about five. A dim wintry light filtered into my room. The wind howled outside. The curtains at my windows fluttered like ghosts, the shades rattled. I heard my parents talking in the kitchen, in low voices which sometimes erupted loud and hoarse. My father, unshaven, with a stubbly black growth, dark circles under eyes that were wild and feverish, a face drawn and yellow from lack of sleep, stood in the kitchen doorway. He was wearing his heavy winter garments and was on the verge of departure.

My mother, wrapped in a plaid flannel bathrobe, sat at the kitchen table, head resting on its surface, hands covering her head as if to shut out the world, or to shield herself from a blow, from pain. She was sobbing quietly.

Huddled in blankets, I sat up in bed. My sister was sound asleep in the nearby crib. I heard my mother and father talking.

"I'm going," he said.

"You just came and now you're going," she answered.

"Please, Bella, I'm sorry. It won't happen again. I promise."

My mother's shoulders shook convulsively, I heard her muffled sobs.

"I couldn't come home earlier," said my father. "I was losing too much and had a hunch I'd make a comeback if I played longer. And I was right. My luck changed. The game turned around for me, I got a flush and won a big pot, thirty-seven dollars . . ."

My mother raised her head and I saw that it was bound in a wet, white handkerchief as for headache. She emitted a prolonged *Ooooh*, interrupting my father's words, or perhaps releasing an outcry too long stifled. I recoiled from that cry and stuffed the blanket into my mouth.

"Shhh," said my father. "You'll wake up the children."

My mother spoke in a low voice, a monotone, as if in her sleep. "I don't believe you, I don't believe you. You lost again. I can tell from your face. A whole night out, gambling. You promised you wouldn't."

"I couldn't help it. I went to the game straight after work, for only an hour, but I got stuck. You know how it is."

"It's always the same. One hour leads to two hours, leads to all night."

My father gazed at her haggardly. "Go to bed, Bella.

It's still so early . . . Are the children all right . . .? Do you have a headache?"

My mother ignored his questions. Her voice grew accusing, berating, yet overlaid with pity. "Look at you. Unshaved, exhausted. You look like a consumptive. How can you go to work in this condition, without sleep, hanging from windows up on those high floors?" Her tone softened but grew more urgent. "Joe, I beg you, phone your customers and tell them you'll come and clean their windows tomorrow. You're too sleepy to go to work, you'll fall . . ."

"I can't, Bella. Tomorrow there's other work, and I'll never be able to catch up. Customers don't want to hear excuses . . . We have so many bills."

"All night you gamble and lose a fortune, and then slave all day with sweat and guts for a lousy couple of dollars, hanging from windows in this icy cold, fingers frozen in water . . ."

"Bella, we're lucky to pay our bills."

"It's blood money!"

"At least I'm my own boss and have no one to answer to."

"You answer to the devil!"

"Bella, please!"

"One day you'll fall to the sidewalk and the police will call me like they did two years ago. That time you were lucky—you fell from the second floor . . ."

"The window hooks were defective."

My mother shook her head over and over, as if to chase a persistent fly. "What will happen to me and the children if you die?"

"Bella, please, nothing is going to happen to me. I'm tough." He went over and held her shoulder. She didn't move. He stood behind her, laid his hands on either side of her head, rubbing the temples. "Does it hurt very bad?"

Suddenly my mother let out a strange sound, a wail, a combined lament and cry of anger. "I . . . I hurt so much!"

His hands dropped again to her shoulder like useless weight. "Stay home, Joe. I'm afraid you'll be killed."

"I can't, I told you. I'll try to come home early."

"You're dead tired."

"I'll sleep when I come home . . . Can I get you some aspirins?"

My mother's head shot up. I couldn't see her face, but I imagined her eyes, flashing, and with a frightening look. "Get me some poison! That's what you can get me. I curse the day I met you. I curse the day I came to this country. I curse the day I was born!"

"Bella, you know how I love you!"

"What good does it do? It's a love that kills."

"I'm a good husband. Faithful, a good provider. Our children have everything."

"You'll kill us with kindness. And gambling will kill you."

"I promise I'm going to change. I'll stop playing cards. We'll save every penny we can. I'll buy a large route and clean only storefronts, no buildings. I won't have to climb windows. I'll prosper and hire other men. You won't have to worry about my falling. Bella, I promise. Things will get better."

And then I heard my mother answer in a voice barely audible: "You've promised before."

"This time I really mean it."

"It's a demon in you, Joseph, a dybbuk. When you sit at the table and hear the shuffle of cards, the sound of chips, you forget everything. It's a fever. Gambling

comes before me, before the children . . . before yourself. You haven't bought yourself a pair of shoes in
years. You never take a vacation. The money you earn
is blood money. And you gamble it away like paper.
You're a lost soul."

"People can change . . ."

"You're destroying us. Sometimes I wish it were all
over."

"Don't talk that way. How can you talk like that? A
mother of two beautiful children, one that you're still
nursing."

"She's suckling bitter milk."

"Bella, I have to leave. Go back to bed."

"So go already," my mother snapped, and wrenched
herself free from his hands, which were still resting on
her shoulder. His own shoulders drooped. His features
sagged. With head bowed, he trailed out of the kitchen. I
heard the front door closing. My mother, still seated,
rocked back and forth on her chair, holding her head as
if to prevent it from bursting.

Then I heard her cry out in a high falsetto voice,
almost like a child's. "Oh, why? Why?"

I burrowed my head under the quilt.

After a while, I uncovered myself to breathe. The
light in the room had gradually brightened. It was
dawn. My mother rose and swayed slightly by her
chair. She grasped the back to steady herself. The
house was still, so still you could hear the small sleeping sounds of my sister in her crib. I saw my mother
walk over to the window and stand motionless for several moments, staring outside. The grating of the window guard looked like iron claws balancing scoops of
snow. Then she turned, crossed the kitchen, and
padded barefoot into our room. I pretended to be

asleep. She moved first to the crib, rearranging the blanket on my sister, and stood for several moments gazing at her. Then she came over to my bed and drew the cover away from my face. I kept my eyes clamped shut. I felt her hand passing lightly over the quilt and the hump of my body. Then I heard her steps leaving our bedroom. I opened my eyes. She had returned to the kitchen window. Outside, the wind was screeching like a siren. I wondered where my father was. My mother kept staring out the window as if hypnotized. Was she looking across the alley into the neighbor's kitchen? Or down at the ground? The father of a boy in our building had jumped from the roof last winter, and even after they'd rubbed the sidewalk with sand the spot where he fell remained a rusty red. When my friends and I played hopscotch we could see it. After a while, my mother began nodding her head, like people do when they've reached a decision. I bolted upright in bed, unobserved, and with my eyes glued on her, began chewing nervously on my fingers. My mother was motionless as in a game of freeze. At last she turned from the window. A terrible hopeless look was on her face, the sort of expression people allow themselves only when they're alone. With the slow steps of a sleepwalker, she moved from the kitchen into her bedroom. The wooden floor of the hallway between the rooms creaked underfoot. I could no longer see or hear her. Abandoned, in panic, I jumped from my bed. The baby let out a little squeak in her sleep.

I ran across the cold linoleum of the kitchen and down the hall toward my parents' bedroom. From the door, I saw their bed. Empty. A shaft of weak sunlight shrouded the floor. I let out a tattered sob, like the sound a puppy makes when you've inadvertently stepped on its tail. For a moment, I stood immobile, hands clenched at my sides, eyes closed. Then I raced through the doorway of their bedroom.

My mother was standing with her back to the door in front of the window. She didn't see or hear me. She was absorbed in trying to raise the sash, which was stuck. She struggled. I heard little puffs of exertion. The wood creaked in the silence. At last the window edged open an inch.

"Mama!"

My mother swung around, eyes bulging. Her face was a ghostly white under its white headache band. I ran over and clutched her around the waist.

"*Maidele*, what's the matter?"

"What are you doing, Mama?"

"Go back to bed. Come, I'll take you."

"Mama, I'm afraid."

"Shh," she said, holding me against her and smoothing my hair. My head barely reached to her belly. I buried my face in its warmth and softness. I closed myself in her deep maternal smell.

Without raising my head, I asked, "Why are you opening the window?"

"Foolish child," she said in Yiddish. "*Narishe kindt*, I open it every day to air the pillows. See? Come, help me, and then go back to bed. It's still very early, and cold. The heat isn't up yet."

I trailed her to their bed; she lifted the two pillows, hers and my father's, and set them out on the open window. "There. Now let's take you back to bed."

I burst out crying.

Like phantoms without footsteps, we glided soundlessly through the dim light across the bedroom, through the kitchen, into my room. She tucked me into bed, kissed me, returned to the kitchen. I heard her moving to the sink, turning on the tap. Air sputtered in the pipe a few moments, then water gushed forth. She removed the white handkerchief from her head, wet it under the rush of water, turned off the tap, wrung out the handkerchief, and once again bound it around her forehead. She knotted it tightly. Then she turned and stared at the kitchen table, the high chair, the spot in the doorway where my father had stood. She moved to the window in slow motion, stood in front of it, and looked out longingly.

And then there was her asthma. It started with hay fever one summer in Monticello. She must have been in her early thirties. The sneezing recurred a second season, accompanied this time by shortness of breath. When the ragweed and goldenrod faded, the sneezing subsided, the asthma continued.

I'd sit opposite her at the kitchen table, eyes glued on her face, red and contorted from its straining and wheezing, pumping medicine into her mouth through a small gray rubber inhalator which she now always carried in her purse. Sometimes an attack came very fast. Her eyes would bulge, her lips went dry. She'd signal me to fetch her inhalator and pills. There was a terrible urgency. Nothing else mattered except this crisis of suffocation. I felt frantic and helpless, watching her gasp for breath. I would have exhaled my own into her if I could.

An allergist told her she was allergic to ragweed, mold, dust, nuts, chocolate, spinach, animal fur, aspirin. She avoided all these inciters, removed the dust-collecting curtains from her room, took injections for a few years to desensitize herself. But the attacks persisted and increased in frequency. She sought another doctor. He asked her if she smoked. She didn't. Try, he said, and gave her a prescription for a certain medical cigarette obtainable at the drugstore: cannabis. When you inhaled deeply, it was supposed to dilate the bronchi. The tobacco, on being lit, exuded an odd sweet smell. Bella puffed away, but it didn't work. "Maybe I'm not inhaling deep enough," she said, but finally gave up. Years, many years later, I recognized that familiar sweet herbal odor when a musician at a midnight jazz session in a loft on West Twenty-eighth Street lit a joint and passed it around. Bella was the first pot smoker I knew.

Someone told her about a certain practitioner who'd devised a successful cure for asthma. I accompanied her on a long circuitous subway trip to a remote neighborhood in Brooklyn. We boarded unfamiliar BMT's, halted at stations with strange-sounding names, each of which looked like a wrong stop, dismounted in a dingy, provincial section that seemed like a foreign country. In the musty ground-floor office of a Victorian house we sat in the doctor's waiting room, hemmed in by dark furniture and lace curtains. He examined my mother, took an X ray of her chest, sent her away with three bottles of red medicine of his own concoction to take three times a day. He instructed her to buy an oversize inhalator, which she was to fill with the medicine and use routinely, as well as during an attack. The heavy, bulky, costly apparatus was set up permanently on a table in our foyer. It had wide, long tubes, which my mother attached to a mask on her face, and knobs to set it into motion. The machine made a whirring sound while in operation and vibrated on the table. The spray let off a dense iodine odor. I can still see her, mask over her face, inhaling laboriously, perspiration beading her forehead. During attacks, she seemed far away, concentrating solely on luring back the fugitive air. We heard her panting for air. My little sister stood off a bit, hands dangling by her side. Eventually the machine provided relief. My mother's face emerged. She clicked off the dial, looking exhausted, like someone who has finished an arduous race. Her hands were cold, her face pale. She sat for a moment and then went for a glass of water. It was over. But we knew there would be another time.

In my fifteenth year, it became difficult for me, too, to catch my breath. It was the year I began going out with boys. I kept my problem secret. I'd stand in front of the window, in my room or the living room, pretending to look out, and feel that tightening in my chest. The air seemed like a lead wall closing in on me. I stared out at the quilted sky, licked my lips, and inhaled sharply. To sneak up on breath, catch it unawares. My chest heaved unnaturally, providing no relief. Then, without pause, and contrary to the normal breathing rhythm, I tried to grope for it another way, slowly, deeply. I'd inhale, making no sound, imitating the breathing movement, but no air would enter. Air was for others. Not for my mother, or myself. I yawned as if to broaden the entrance to my lungs, picturing a live carp with its eyes popping, its mouth agape as the fish seller cudgeled it over its head.

Imitating the deep-breathing exercises in gym, I'd raise my arms high over my head, describe a wide circle outward, to give my lungs space, then down to my sides and up again to complete the arc. Out with the bad air, in with the good, as the gym teacher would say. But my body remained tight and constricted like a drum. My windpipe was an inflexible, clogged hose. No matter what effort I made, elusive oxygen was blocked from my body.

If the shortness of breath occurred while I was in bed, I'd prop myself against the pillows and try to think of something else, reasoning that breathing, after all, was an automatic function, and that if you didn't pay attention, the body would take over and perform involuntarily. I'd pick up a book, pretend to read. When that didn't work, I'd turn and get on all fours, letting my head hang loose between arms and knees and shoulders.

I was certain that I was destined to be an asthmatic. Doctors said the tendency was inherited. A new doctor would invariably ask my mother if anyone in her family had suffered from the same complaint. Not as far as she knew.

My difficulty lasted for one spring and one summer. During that summer we were vacationing at the seashore, where the pollen count was low. It was in Rockaway. I'd flee to the boardwalk in search of air. I'd lean over the rail looking out at the sea and jetty, at the incoming and outgoing tide. Just one breath, I'd beg silently, just one satisfying breath. The damp salt breeze sprayed my face as I stalked the promenade or clutched the rail, waiting for air to come with the tide.

As mysteriously as my mother's asthma began, so did it vanish. For about fifteen years it plagued her, and then subsided. Years after, unable to believe that it had truly gone, she carried that little rubber inhalator in her purse, just in case. She held on to the bulky breathing apparatus until they moved away from that Bronx apartment some ten years later.

When I was young I had a few secrets of my own. Among them, the way that my father earned his living and that both my parents were poker sharks. How could I dare reveal to my conventional friends that one night at around midnight two police detectives came knock-knocking at our door and that I myself, Little Red Ridinghood, let them in? How can I describe that wild scramble of the players as they hurried to hide the chips and the deck, to pretend they were merely holding a friendly Saturday night get-together?

Why was my father different from other fathers? So private, ungregarious, preferring his newspaper and family, or the gaming table, to an innocent night of pinochle with the boys? And why wasn't my mother like the other good ladies on our block who sat on wooden chairs in front of the house and gossiped and knitted after they'd finished their cleaning, marketing, and ironing? Why didn't she show up at Open School Week?

Why did my mother, after finishing her household tasks, hurry off for an afternoon game? Why did she go back to sleep after dispatching me to school if not to catch up on sleep lost during a nocturnal bout at the card table? I couldn't face the fact of my parents' gambling. Even in the diary of my thirteenth year, I euphemized my mother's sorties as "going to see her friends." On the other hand, I was savvy enough to ask at dinnertime when she came home, "Did you win?" My mother went to play poker as others went to work.

She worked part-time: certain afternoons, occasional
evenings. Her earnings supplemented my father's, perhaps freed her from pinching pennies.

And then there were those evenings when "friends"
came to our house. The big green felt pad stored in the
foyer closet was unfolded on the dining-room table, and
a white damask cloth unfurled on top. I suppose that is
why we held on to that staid massive table with its ten
straight-backed chairs all those years, certainly not for
formal dining, but for card games. Two new slippery
decks of Tally-Ho cards, one red, the other blue, which
I perhaps had been sent to fetch from Penrod's Station-
ery Store on the Avenue, lay on the table in crisp, slippery readiness. Sometimes my sister and I would peel
the cellophane wrapper from the decks and remove the
jokers in advance—we were forming our own special
deck of jokers. In dribs and drabs, the guests began
arriving. They'd pinch our cheeks, my sister's and mine,
and lay their coats on the double bed in my parents'
room.

There were gaming housewives, a chiropodist who
wore green gaiters on his shirtsleeves and chewed on a
frayed cigar, a taxicab driver who called everyone
"Kiddo" and would occasionally pinch-hit by driving a
stranded player home to some distant neighborhood, a
chiropractor who instructed my mother to give me
plenty of rare steak and cabbage to "build her up" in
my convalescence from pneumonia and bronchitis, a
real "swell" who arrived in mink coat with a pair of
knockout cocktail rings on her scarlet-tipped fingers, a
Mrs. Levine who ran a fish store on Allerton Avenue, a
dentist's wife from classy Cabrini Boulevard, a Mrs.
Tepler who had an epileptic daughter, and a certain

Harold and Sam who always wore jackets and ties and whose principal occupation seemed to be poker.

My sister and I never hung around very long past the initial "cut" and "you deal." There was sort of an unwritten rule, a decorum which kept youngsters at bay from a table in action where the stakes were high. But from our room we'd hear the steady shuffle of cards, the click of chips, the calls "pass," "straight flush," "full house," "your deal," "a pair of aces." Sparks of excitement, tension, and concentration fizzled behind the lace-curtained French doors of our dining room.

My mother preferred the heady atmosphere of the table to the tame gossip of housewives, bargain hunting, or window-shopping. She enjoyed the mix of players, liked their temperaments—they were amusing and liberal, a great virtue in her eyes. None of my friends knew about my parents' avocation.

My mother's accent was another source of shame for me. When I was seventeen and intent upon rising above the circumstances of my immigrant background, I shied away from introducing her to my Harvard date, a law student from a third-generation American Park Avenue family whose father worked on Wall Street. My mother suddenly seemed so plain, as plain as a Hoover apron, her inflection so unmistakably Yiddish. In later years, I was proud of her, insistent that she join us at home, with friends, filmmakers, writers, whoever was there.

I recall particularly one Sunday after a family dinner, we were sitting in the living room when the phone rang. It was Rainer Werner Fassbinder, the German director. He'd just arrived in town for the New York Film Festival, which was premiering his latest film. My husband invited him to drop by, quite expecting him to decline. This is a man noted for his reserve, his meager threshold for social amenities, his brusqueness with all but the closest intimates. He'd been known to sit at a luncheon in his honor in stony silence, to fail to show up for social engagements, to be rude. To my husband's surprise, Fassbinder accepted the invitation and asked if he might bring a friend.

My husband hung up, casually mentioning that Fassbinder was coming by in half an hour, and we, scarcely noticing, resumed the thread of our conversation. Shortly after, my mother indicated that she was tired and would be leaving. She didn't look a bit tired. It was her tactful way of not intruding. We insisted that she stay, though privately I had my fingers crossed that she wouldn't be witness to some predictable curtness at worst, a stiff encounter at best. The man whose movies were caustic satires of every institution up and down the line, families not excluded, could not be counted on to be nice to your mama.

Fassbinder was punctual. He and his friend arrived on the dot, in their matching black leather pants and leather zippered jackets. We introduced them to my mother and our daughters. Both men spoke fluent English. Then, the usual queries one makes to a foreign visitor: When did you arrive? How was the flight? How long will you stay? The replies were brief. A conversation with Fassbinder required a slow massage to get underway. Fassbinder, on a chair, and my husband, on the sofa, proceeded to speak in low tones about his next project, while I engaged his friend, a lively slender man from Frankfurt who'd done a variety of things, ranging from owning a florist shop to running a bar. Bella and the girls talked to each other. Soon they drifted off, Bella to hear Emily play a new Liszt piece on the piano, Nina and Sarah to their rooms. From the living room we heard the scattered theme of the sonata.

In a short while, Bella returned, seated herself in that calm, settled way of hers, listened in on my conversation with Fassbinder's friend, and was drawn into it.

In a lull, Fassbinder turned to my mother, asked her where she lived, how many children she had, where she came from originally. Not too many transitions, rather abrupt in that way of his. I nearly fainted. Never had I heard him actively initiate so much conversation at one clip. My mother replied easily, unselfconsciously. Soon the girls returned, one sat on the arm of Bella's chair, the others on the window seat, gazing discreetly but curiously at the prodigious director, the Lope de Vega of film. They'd seen his brilliant and outrageous *The Bitter Tears of Petra von Kant* and his moving *Ali: Fear Eats the Soul*.

The visit was drawing to an end. The two men had an appointment downtown. Fassbinder rose to his feet in that rather jolting way of his—he'd not removed his leather jacket. We stood up to say good night. He approached my mother, who was still seated, took her hand, kissed it, and told her how happy he was to meet her. My mother smiled her gentle smile and thanked him.

The next morning, Fassbinder called my husband to say how touched he was to have been invited into "the heart of your family." Seldom did he come into people's homes, meet their children and mothers.

So, even this "terrorist" was accessible. His presumed Teutonic arrogance was perhaps largely shyness. In the face of Bella, you couldn't be cruel. Her lack of artifice, her wiseness, her humanness were apparent.

In his late fifties, my father, while working, slipped on a faulty sidewalk grating, fell, lost consciousness briefly, and was thereafter different. Following the accident, he seemed disoriented and restless. I accompanied him to a neurologist, an elderly doctor on whose wall hung two photographs, one of Albert Einstein, the other of the Indian poet Tagore, both friends of his. The doctor diagnosed my father's condition. Parkinson's disease.

The symptoms were neurologically evident, though at that point barely discernible. The typical hasty walk, body tilted forward, a certain masklike expression and muscular rigidity, a tremor of the left hand, a dryness of the mouth, a restlessness that drives the patient ceaselessly from spot to spot. The doctor prescribed pills to still the trembling, warm baths to relax the muscles, and advised, if possible, a benign climate in winter. He chatted with us, asked my father if by chance he'd ever had encephalitis—apparently it was sometimes a catalyst of Parkinson's, and there'd been an epidemic of it in Europe around World War I. My father thought not. The doctor engaged my father in conversation, inquiring into his life, nodding at the pride he showed in his children, showing him the attention, humanness, and compassion which doctors seldom have time for. He was tacitly encouraging him to face the difficulties of a chronic affliction whose scope the rest of us did not anticipate. At one point, he led us to a corner where a poem of Tagore hung on the wall, and asked if I'd read it aloud.

Finally, we were sent off with samples of medication and told to return whenever we needed more. That good man did not detail for us the downward path of that eroding disease. He said nothing to discourage my father. He focused, not on the affliction, but on the affirmative totality of my father's life.

In the following fifteen years, my father was transformed from a powerful, vigorous, upright individual into a bent, frail, teetering man. His stride, which I could barely keep up with as a child, became halting and jerky. Those powerful long-fingered hands only ceased their quivering when he slept or when he held one with the other. And they were always cold. As were his feet. His clear gray eyes, which used to zoom in on us for childhood pranks, were now vague. The deterioration of the optic muscles caused him great difficulty in reading those newspapers over which he used to pore with the zeal of an archivist. Reading became frustration. His face, once so expressive, now displayed a masked, dazed expression. His eyes acquired a deep omniscience, an enigmatic and at the same time a tender look. The facial muscles could not register a show of temper, or response to jokes he would have wanted to laugh at. But worst of all was that restlessness, that agitation which drove him from place to place. Laboriously, he'd climb into bed only to climb out immediately, sit down only to stand up, pace the small apartment as if eternally searching for something. It was as though a dybbuk would not let his body be, endlessly prodding it on. This inquietude never improved; it grew worse. The progression was gradual during the first ten years of its course, then more accelerated in the last three. He became an invalid.

Always he rebelled against the medication, which calmed the muscles but made the head drowsy. After taking it, he'd sit at times in his armchair as if in a daze or a trance. All his life he'd hated medicine, believed that natural cures were the morally correct ones. My sister and I would have to negotiate with him as children to take aspirin for headaches. And now he was a prisoner of pills. At one point he made up his mind to abandon them once and for all. That day, he lay on his bed, his whole body tossing convulsively. It frightened my mother and, tragically, convinced him. He was enslaved to pills.

At one time, I learned of a surgical procedure that had been used with some success in the treatment of Parkinson's disease. A needle would pierce the brain, an icy trickle then probe the nerve that was the seat of the agitation, and freeze it. I convinced my father to explore the possibility of undergoing the operation. We went uptown to St. Barnabas Hospital. A neurologist examined him, explained the procedure, indicated that it could reduce the tremor. My father scrutinized patients who sat stonily in the corridor, people who'd undergone the operation. Their gaze was vegetative. They seemed frighteningly calm. Stilled. My father said no.

Joseph was a proud man. Stubborn, too. Though his gait was unsteady, he refused to the end to use a cane or a metal walker. Always an avid perambulator, he persisted in those solitary walks, holding one hand with the other to halt the shaking. Sometimes he fell. A passerby would help him to his feet. I don't know how many times that happened. He didn't talk about it. Once he stumbled on a curbstone and an ambulance came and took him to the hospital. I was at home and received a call: "This is Sergeant Walker of the 23rd Precinct. Are you the daughter of Joseph Tolpen?" Oh no, he's dead, I thought. "Well, your father's had an accident and is at the Emergency Room of Knicker-bocker Hospital."

I found him there, dazed, huddled on a bench, his cheekbone black-and-blue, his lips purplish, drawn, and dry. His eyes flickered with relief and happiness to see me, also with remorse and humiliation. "I was out for a walk," he said softly. His eyes filled with tears. I'd never seen him so forlorn, and broken. I helped him undress so that the doctor could examine him. His knees and shins were bruised, his arms and legs so bony that every articulation in his skeleton showed through its scant covering of flesh. My father. That once beauti-ful, rounded, muscular physique now fragile and wasted. Tossed by that eternal agitation with its merci-less burning of calories. As I helped him out of the taxi in front of their building, he uttered almost inaudi-bly, in Yiddish, "Woe is me."

My mother tended him. She accepted this *umglick*, this bad luck, as one accepts a bad hand dealt in a game of cards, a hand, nevertheless, that had to be played. She accepted it the way a mother might accept the misfortune of a handicapped child. She had great pity for him. Coaxed him to swallow the dreaded pills, prepared the most nourishing foods to give him strength—freshly squeezed orange juice, oatmeal sprinkled with sweet cream. She made the dishes he loved—lamb stews, rice puddings, bowls of fresh peaches and berries and sour cream, corn muffins. Simple foods that were easy to chew, for his teeth were no longer his own. His needs were trying. His sleep fitful. All during the night he kept awakening, with that impetus to move, to get out of bed, go to the bathroom, prowl. He endured with a minimum of rest. The disease goaded him on, a bizarre source of energy. That endless agitation gave him no respite, and her barely any. He'd rove from room to room, get underfoot while she was working in the kitchen, require help getting into bed and finding a comfortable position, only to feel impelled almost at once to get out of bed. He tracked the house, propelled by an uncontrollable force. Sometimes it drove even my patient mother to exasperation. At around four in the morning he needed breakfast. It was as if that nocturnal activity produced an appetite. He didn't arouse my mother, but she'd hear him puttering in the kitchen and would get out of bed, cook some cereal for him, prepare some toast and tea, then go back to sleep. He realized how that endless motion of his got on her nerves, but the poor man couldn't stop. He also knew that her impatience was temporary, her caring and compassion steadfast. Their relationship had extended beyond physical desire, mating, child rearing, homemaking, into that deepest realm of empathy. Bella was his lover, his mother, his sister, his other.

Summers, he'd come to visit us in the country. It relieved my mother of her round-the-clock nursing and responsibility. He came enthusiastically, for he loved the trees, the water views, the endless luminous skies of Long Island, those long, contemplative walks that he now took at a slow pace, up the road, circling, then back to our property. I'd prepare my mother's dishes, stand beside him in the shower to make sure he didn't slip, help him to wash, assist him in that trying ritual of climbing into bed at night and finding a comfortable position. He loved being with us, but within ten days yearned to go home, to be with my mother. At that point my mother would join us.

Perhaps two years before he died, his rigidity worsened and it became increasingly difficult for him to get in and out of chairs, bed, the bathtub, to dress and undress. My mother had to lift him, dress him; she did it all. There were dark circles under her eyes from the strain. The doctor warned her that her uterus was extremely low, pressing against her bladder, that she required surgery, that she must abstain from lifting, carrying, pushing, pulling. Under the physical strain, her patience grew shorter. Exactly at the time that my father's demands grew greater. The doctor gave his professional advice. My father's condition would only deteriorate. There was no realistic way for her to tend him. It would be better for him, and her, if he were in a nursing home. There male nurses could assist him, bathe him. The hallways were fitted with rails, constant medical supervision was available, also physical therapy. The home the doctor had in mind was in the country, it had a solarium, my father would have easy access to the outdoors. There were interesting activities—concerts, lectures, films. It was a most humane place.

So convincingly did he present the case, so precarious was my mother's physical condition, that we, too, urged her and my father to consider it. Deep down, my father hated the idea. For him, home was the core of his life, and home meant my mother. Perhaps he thought that the only way to withstand his affliction, the burden of living, was to be under the same roof with her, to have his children and grandchildren visit as often as possible. Nothing else mattered except to be with those you loved. As for concerts, lectures, or films, he preferred his own meditations. But. Aware of my mother's physical condition, he acquiesced. And, out of sheer exhaustion, she did, too.

We made all the arrangements. Drove them up to the beautiful nursing home in Westchester County. Excellent facilities, highly sanitary, landscaped with trees and shrubbery, presided over by doctors and nurses, social workers, cheerful uniformed attendants. My father lasted there ten days. On our first visit, he was quite silent, didn't complain about the schedule, the food, about anything, in fact. When we drove home, my mother was silent, too. She looked deeply troubled. Untypically, she did not articulate what was on her mind. We all felt guilty, because we knew he did not want to be there.

Three days later my mother phoned. Would I drive her up to the nursing home to pick up my father? He had phoned, implored her to take him home. She did not resist, and would not hear of my suggestions for postponement. She did not even want to wait until tomorrow. That afternoon we drove up. He was ready. Sitting in his spotless room, alongside the bed with its adjustable bars, his suitcase packed.

The matter was never discussed again. He never left her. She never uttered a peep of complaint. Once she committed herself to his care, her devotion was endless. He never lost total mobility, was not confined to a wheelchair, did not become incontinent. Somehow, she managed. He died several years later in his own bed, of a pneumonia which lasted two days. An hour before he drew his last breath, my mother spooned some warm cereal into his mouth. He told her he enjoyed it. When he closed his eyes, she was the last thing he saw. "My golden Bleema," he said.

After he died she went for the long-postponed operation to boost her insides, to raise her sagging organs. In later years, she often said: "No matter how sick he was, and how hard it was, I miss him. I don't care how many friends you have, how good your children are, your husband is your closest friend."

A distinguishing characteristic of the human mammal: the prolonged dependency of the offspring on maternal protection. All mothers are not motherly. Some motherly mothers are overprotective. Trespassers on their children's lives. Refusing to let go.

Bella was motherly, but not overprotective. Though not a modern woman with professional ambitions, she was modern in the leeway she gave her daughters. She did not creep into our skins, poke into our affairs, dispute our goals. She was not involved in our homework, or reading lists, and exhibited small concern over grades, assured that we were doing our best and that no teacher could therefore condemn us. We chose our own clothes when we were still quite young. My mother did not try, as some parents nowadays do, to be our peer, to dress as we did, or "pick up" on our language. She was not competitive with our youth, nor did she make us feel guilty about it. Though friendly with our friends, she was not overly chummy. She did not inquire solicitously, or intrusively, into each of our activities, our social forays, what was going on in our heads. We were allowed the space and privacy to grow up.

Though she gave us ample rope, if at any point she found an adventure unacceptable, she didn't hesitate to lasso us in with a loud no. "No is no," she'd say, "even if you stand on your head." We heard it often enough. There was nothing evasive about those messages.

"Don't bring home a little bastard," she told me without a blink.

My mother's world was different from mine. That was clear. To her and to me. Her world, I dreamed of transcending. It was her wish as well. She knew her limitations, understood the source of those limitations, knew that certain deprivations were irrevocable, but held no one to blame. Bella understood herself in her own existence.

My mother did not have extravagant expectations of us, driving ambitions to live her life through ours. Her ultimate caution was to "take care of yourself," and her great wish, that we be happy. It was my father who yearned for us to "be somebody." His emphasis on education was old as the Jews, and his faith in America and the immigrant vision vast.

I did not experience many of the typical generational conflicts with my parents, because our differences were so clear. They were European immigrants, focused on economic survival, health, the haven of family. I understood their struggle, would gaze at length at a price tag, mentally calculating how many pre-dawn hours of my father's toil went into the purchase of a winter coat. I felt a certain protectiveness toward my parents that frustrated any tumultuous impulses of adolescent rebellion. Ours was an old-style family. There were no boundary confusions between mother and daughter, no fuzzy lines. She recognized that our ways were different from hers. For her, those matters were less important than character and being yourself in your own life.

Bella in many ways was the ideal traditional mother. All-giving, all-forgiving, all-caring, all-dedicated. The children came first.

Mothers serve as models for their daughters. A

grown daughter thinks, What would she have wanted? What would she have done? When she is acting contrary to her mother's presumed desire, the daughter's anxiety is aroused. Loss of mother's approval still matters.

Unwittingly, Bella may have pressed me too far in my own motherliness. I was trying to emulate that old pattern. To be the perfect mother. At the same time, I did not want to lose the thread of the individual I was before motherhood. Not to betray my true self. Result: conflict and guilt often nagged intrusively at my work.

It was a juggling act. To nurse and, in between nursings, hurry off to a class. To lay a child in for her nap, then sneak off to a quiet corner to translate, write, or read, ear always cocked for some untoward infantile squeak. To outline a project, and simultaneously keep an eye on a bevy of toddlers jousting in the next room. In my mind, I was always in two places at once. "You can't be at two weddings with one backside," she used to say. But I always was. Niggling twinges of you-should-be-somewhere-else accompanied research in the library stacks, or some unforeseen homecoming delay. When I read and knew the children were idle—maybe, God forbid, bored—I'd needle myself with the thought: I ought to be reading to *them*. One thinks: A mother should be with her children. Always providing, enriching, nourishing. Personal pursuits can wait.

Bella identified herself primarily as a mother. This realization prompts me to reflect: Did I adequately repay her? Is my grief in part a sense of something owed her? What will I expect of my daughters when I am old?

Summertime. Oh, summertime. Summer hibernation. Like a wounded animal, I slink into seclusion from the business of the world, to lick my wounds, to lick where it hurts. Before leaving the city, I phone my sister. How are you doing? Come and visit. Call if you need anything.

Our daughters are in their different places. Oddly, I do not miss them. The empty nest is a relief. I feel freed, wanting to be alone, and with her. To maintain steadfast contact with her. My husband understands. He is there, but lets me mourn.

We open the musty country house. Ample and gentle as a lap, this bulky weathered clapboard house of ours, with its bleached blue trim on which rain marks and sun streaks are ingrained like dried tears. It sits on a grassy knoll that runs down to the bay in wide slopes. Ivy swaddles the chimney and overruns the flagstone path. The porte-cochere shelters our ancient wicker swing, and the eaves of the porch a barn swallow's abandoned nest. Upstairs, behind attic dormers, slumber old dollhouses, children's games and shell collections gathering cobwebs. We enter. The smell of mildew, droppings of mice, new cracks in the walls, water spots on the ceiling—traces of the ceaseless heaving and activity in a house winter unoccupied.

Here, everywhere, I find signs of Bella. A black bobby pin, hers, lies where it fell last Thanksgiving on the green planks of the bathroom floor. Her toothbrush, shaggy from vigorous brushings, stands upright in the common family glass. Her jar of cold cream is in the medicine cabinet. Intimate objects left by one who comes to a house and goes away, but means to return.

In the kitchen, three sleek black pots with long metal handles hang on hooks over the stove. She dragged me into town that Thanksgiving weekend and insisted on buying them. Did she have a premonition? Metal lasts. The corner hutch where we store our stemware still surely holds her fingerprints. I remember that rainy end-of-November afternoon when I came in and found her removing the glasses, piece by piece, washing them, drying them, replacing them.

I enter her bedroom and stand by the empty bed. Fresh pain.

I've brought two photographs of her which I hang in our bedroom, needing the daily link of her physical image. In one picture, you see her from a distance. She is seated on a wooden-slat chair on the slope by the house overlooking the water. Her legs are crossed, her hands folded in her lap. She is looking out on the water, focused on her thoughts and memories and dreams. Alongside her is an empty chair. My father often sat in that.

The other photograph is a close-up, in the same chair. She is looking straight into the camera. Without artifice. Smiling, lighthearted even, with a trace of humor and shrewdness in her eyes, self-accepting and welcoming.

That distance shot, with its horizontal bands of sky, water, slopes of grass, suggests a serenity, a spirituality, an infiniteness of time and space. I look at it and feel calm and comforted. The close-up, with its tactile sense of features, textures, finiteness, reduces me to tears. Through blurred eyes, I can't see her image.

Checking the garden to see how it withstood winter. The narcissus made it, the jonquils made it, the tulips made it, the peonies made it, the clematis made it, the magnolia made it, the dogwood made it, the rhododendron made it, the wisteria made it, the columbine made it, the lilies of the valley made it, the tarragon made it, the lilacs made it, even the vulnerable azaleas made it. My mother did not make it.

Her summer visits. She slept late. I'd squeeze oranges and leave a glass of juice for her in the refrigerator. I'd set the kettle to simmer in back of the stove and place a cup on the table with a wedge of lemon on its saucer. "You don't have to bother," she'd say. I wanted to.

She rose earlier in the country than in the city; later, however, than the rest of us. Sometimes the girls would deliberately rattle around or squabble outside her door to rouse her. Her face had a morning sweetness, the cheeks puckered with sleep, an air of happiness at waking in our midst. She'd sit at the edge of her bed for some minutes, didn't rush into the day.

Hot water and lemon, orange juice, coffee. That was her breakfast. Then, still in housecoat and slippers, she went out and sat in the sun on that wooden-slat chair overlooking the water. She'd watch our resident swans and their season's cygnets, the nuns of the Villa Maria convent strolling and saying their beads on the opposite bank, two towheaded boys paddling by in a glistening silver canoe, a gull diving for a fish. My daughters, sometimes singly, at times in pairs, would perch on the arm of her chair and talk, fool around, confide, giggle, poke her ribs, get hugged. Around noon, she went upstairs to bathe. The bath was her supreme pleasure. She seldom missed it. Even on low days, hot water revived her.

After dressing, she'd walk the grounds, admire the trees as if they were progeny, the mimosa in pink feathery bloom, the mulberry heavy with plundering birds, the spindly weeping birch, the dwarf Japanese maple, the peach, the contorted apple tree with its questionable apples. "One is more beautiful than the other," Bella would remark in Yiddish, applying to the trees an expression generally reserved for her grandchildren.

She lingered long by the lilacs, those cascades of double French blooms with their deep pink cast and exquisite fragrance. Lilacs had always been her favorite flower. On Mother's Day when I was ten, I bought her a bunch, they were the first of the season, and she ooh'd and ah'd. The next day I came down with chicken pox. She drew all the shades and set the vase of lilacs in my room to perfume the darkness.

Another time, when my sister and I were quite young, and walking with her in Bronx Park, we saw a mass of superb lilac bushes flowering on a knoll alongside the path. "I want one," said my sister. She, too, was a lilac fan. "You're not supposed to pick the flowers," my mother pointed out. My sister begged. My mother gazed at the imploring face, then at the profusion of blooms. I could almost hear her silently muse: One less flower on the bush won't hurt. She turned and made her way up the gentle embankment crowned with lilacs. At the summit, she reached out and labored to snap off a voluptuous branch. Suddenly a stern voice called out:

"Lady, do you know you're in violation of the law? Picking flowers in the public parks is strictly forbidden." At that moment, the branch snapped and my mother's hand held her guilt aloft. Both my sister and I spun around to a police patrol car with two uniformed officers inside. What were they going to do to my mother? I could imagine visiting her in jail, as in one of those prison movies we saw on Saturday afternoons. "Do you know there's a twenty-five-dollar fine for defacing public property?" he went on. "My little girl wanted just one flower," she said. The two officers glared at our cowering figures, my sister and me, then glanced at each other hopelessly and drove on. Down the hill came my mother, the spray of lilacs in hand, enough blossoms on it for my sister and me to share. Such were the lilacs.

Last, on her walks in the country, Bella would stroll over to the far garden to check on the progress of our grape trellis rampant with purple grapes, and the husky tomatoes, and stoop perhaps to pick a firm, prickly cucumber. She'd examine the little white mushrooms that huddled on an ancient stump, white, moist, infantile.

Summer nights. After dinner, she'd sit outside on the creaky porch swing, alone for a while, soon joined by one of us. Slowly, the others began trickling out. We kept the lights off to discourage the mosquitoes and were often silent, steeped in the nocturnal stirrings of the wind in the trees, the reeds crackling down by the water, the cicadas in their endless sawing. Dizzy with the scent of honeysuckle, we watched the tissue-paper moon drift across that deep summer sky scattered with tinsel stars. The girls came out, noisy often, with their restless energy, their lack of "sitting flesh"—*sitzfleish*, as the Yiddish would have it. Soon they'd drag my mother back into the living room for a game of cards. Her game was full of playfulness and wit. Even in those days when she'd played for stakes, she took risks. Bella taught her grandchildren all the terms, the professional lingo, the banter that card players love. She and the girls bet, bluffed, teased, accused each other of peeking into one another's hand, of cheating. They laughed and kidded each other. The game was a pretext for being together. A backdrop for conversation, along with the record they'd put on and the twang of June bugs and moths striking the window screens.

In every corner of the house I now find a deck of cards. In the drawer of the kitchen table, on the mantel over the fireplace, in the desk, in each of the girl's rooms. Dog-eared decks, decks flecked with pastry and jam stains—sometimes a game began over dessert—and incomplete decks. Incomplete.

The summer house is filled with objects discarded from other places, other times, other lives. Stern mahogany bedroom furniture, now repainted a glossy white, once stood in the bedroom of my deceased in-laws. Incomplete and chipped sets of dishes with faded patterns of childhood, mason jars without tops, ancient can openers and coffee grinders, three-legged chairs with torn cane seats, a vintage Singer sewing machine, empty picture frames, outmoded mini and maxi skirts, torn crab nets, punctured tire tubes, umbrellas with broken ribs, split croquet balls, broken wickers, tennis rackets with missing strings, Japanese sandals minus a center thong, gloves with torn fingers, children's outgrown bathing suits and outworn T-shirts, lamp shades squatting on closet shelves beneath brittle plastic covers, sun-dress patterns ranging from size 2 to size 12, dusty medicine bottles with outdated prescriptions, keys to mysterious locks, broken suitcases bound with spiderwebs, cans of dried-up paint, rusty gardening tools, dried and yellowed historic issues of *The New York Times*, shoes and socks and earrings all minus their mates. Objects lost and never found, wandering through hallways, closets, and attic like souls in purgatory, never reuniting. The old house with its eternally settling walls and ceilings and heaving floors would be bursting at its seams, you'd think, absorbing our past, supporting the artifacts of a family's history, and losses. Children outgrow their clothes. Mothers and fathers drop away. Relentless humans, we persist amid the clutter, the hoarding, the clinging. This summer I shall plant gloxinia, campanula, lupinus, delphinium, gaillardia—only perennials.

Mourning has a path of its own. A route which does not move in one straight line. Some days I can look at her photograph and the image revives her, reinforces her for me. On other days I gaze at her and am blinded with tears. Newly bereft.

What is it that I mourn? Her loss of life? The end of her pleasures? The fact that never again will she drink a glass of sweet country water, or bask in the sun, or set eyes upon her grandchildren, never again steep in a hot bath, or sip a cup of too hot coffee?

Or is it my own loss that I mourn? My insatiability

for her physical presence? The knowledge that she's in the next room, in the next house, in the next city. As when I was a child bedridden with a cold, knowing she was within reach of my voice, that I could bask in her calm, her vigilance and cheer. I could drift in and out of fevers and books and sleep and radio soap operas and cliff-hangers, and she'd still be there. Ready-at-hand.

Or perhaps I mourn the loss of my childhood and youth, of my past. I've lost the witness to my first tooth, my first haircut, my first period, my first bicycle lesson, my first boyfriend, my first fur coat, my first job, my first short story. Only she remembered that plaid blanket on my carriage, only she remembered my measles, my whooping cough, my pneumonia, those mustard plasters, the steaming-over hot kettles for clogged nose and bronchi, the lice she combed from hair infested in school, my flight from the office of Dr. Weissman, that humpbacked monocled dentist who pursued me into the courtyard wielding an instrument that looked like a nutcracker in order to extract a dilatory tooth. I mourn her record of me. Her support, her corroboration, her assurance that when things were bad, they'd get better.

Am I clinging to some youthful version of myself? Or is it my loss of innocence that I mourn? The knowledge that I have changed.

These notes are an umbilical cord. A way of being with her still. Of bringing her close. A release of a deep well of sorrow. Not a work of imagination, with plot or argument, but one of pain. A sharing of pain. A way of absorbing the past, a record of a mutual past, a repository. Their order, like mourning, like memory, does not move in a straight course, in a continuous day-by-day sequence.

Once my daughter Nina at the age of four was weeping bitterly. In trying to comfort her, I brushed the tears from her cheeks. Her sobs immediately converted into an angered outcry: "Give me back my tears!"

Mourning has its ways. As Ovid said, "Truly, it is allowed to weep. By weeping, we disperse our wrath; and tears go through the heart, even like a stream."

Objects are the artifacts of archaeology, also of memory. In last year's nest, I conjure up fledgling barn swallows peering out toward a phantom mother bird fluttering near.

Stepping out of the shower, I glimpse a sparrow perched on the roof, the bird the same color as the gray shingles, and am reminded of that time two summers ago when my husband, with the help of a local workman, reshingled our roof. The two of them were perched up there all day, hammering and shingling away, while Bella on the porch swing below watched their progress and once in a while passed up a couple of cans of ice-cold beer.

The canoe. Today, as we lower our boat from the grass into the bay for its summer launching, other canoe rides of past seasons glide into mind. "Remember how Bella fell out of the canoe?" I hear myself saying to my husband. Strange, but this is the first time I've had the heart to share a memory aloud, and he, following my lead, has tiptoed in sharing his. He smiles, holding the rope as the silvery aluminum bark quivers on hitting the water, and then moors it to its post.

Bella had been sitting in the morning sun that day, still in slippers and house robe, when the girls and I came trooping down the slope on the way to the canoe.

It was one of those shimmering mornings when the dazzle of water is irresistible.

"Come for a canoe ride with us," said the girls.

"I'm not dressed, I haven't had my bath," she protested.

"Oh, come on," they nagged, grabbing her by the hands.

She tilted her head in silent debate with herself and then followed down the hill.

I climbed in first.

"Take off your slippers," said Emily, and held Bella's hand as she stepped from the dock toward the bobbing canoe. The little boat wobbled as it always does on receiving a passenger.

"Stay low," Sarah shouted to Bella, but too late. The boat swayed to one side, Bella veered to an impossible angle and splashed into the water. In a second, the girls were all on their knees on the dock, waiting for her head to bob up, or waiting to jump in after her. Would she be safe, scared, angry? She came up, looking slightly bewildered, a slimy piece of something or other draping her head.

Four pairs of waving hands were extended toward her, mine included. She shook her head and paddled toward the grass. At which point she was willing to accept help in climbing ashore. Her soaked house robe clung to her body, her hair was dripping in her face.

"I'm so sorry, Bella. Are you all right?" Emily looked forlorn.

Sarah seemed uncertain whether to commiserate or giggle. Bella settled it for her. "Sure I'm all right," she said, laughing. "Clumsy and all right." Whereupon she marched herself back onto the dock and once more allowed Emily to help her into the canoe, this time keeping her body properly low as she inched toward her seat.

By the time we'd paddled under the overhead bridge, past the fading mural painted by Nina years back on its stone buttress, visited the nesting place of the swans at a far cove of the inlet, drifted past the old water mill rimmed in pondweed, bladderwort and cattails, waved to the nuns on the shore of the Villa Maria convent, the sun was high and hot, and Bella was dry and poking fun at herself and accusing us of dumping her in the water.

Some of our summers when I was a child were spent on a farm in the Catskills. It was a sprawling place outside South Fallsburg, with cows, a few horses, and vegetables. Farmhands and guests alike ate at a long wooden table in the kitchen. I spent timeless hot days wandering in the hills, pursuing butterflies with my net, picking cucumbers off the vine, flirting with the farmer's teenage son, weaving through the cornfields with my sister and stuffing ourselves with tiny, immature ears of corn, eating cob and all. At mid-afternoon, the farmer's wife laid an outdoor table in a shady grove, a tin pail of buttermilk with thick slabs of homemade bread smeared with honey. In my eleventh summer I fell ignominiously into a manure pile. My first and last. The farmer's son, perched atop the hay wagon, witnessed it and guffawed. I wept in humiliation. My mother scrubbed me in a hot tub, laughed away my tears, and told me it was good luck. That was the summer I caught whooping cough.

Another summer, we spent two weeks at a hotel near

Monticello. Herring and boiled potatoes appeared on the breakfast table. Jackpot slot machines adorned the lobby, and in the casino an ebullient recreation director organized evening entertainments ranging from bingo to amateur shows to circuit comedians. On Children's Night, costumed in blue satin with silver spangles, I performed a tap-dance solo to the tune of "Blue Moon." There was on the property a beautiful natural lake fed by springs and a rushing waterfall. We swam in its ice-cold water, washed our hair with Castile soap beneath the falls. I still dream of diving off that rock into the foaming water, and of my mother gliding in her easy sidestroke beneath the cascade. I stayed in the water so long my fingers would pucker. At night, the young girls lounged on creaky porch rockers gazing futuristically at the immortal starlit sky that glittered frostily against crouching black mountains, and we sang, in high-pitched voices: "I see the moon, and the moon sees me, and the moon sees somebody I want to see. God bless the moon and God bless me, and God bless the somebody I want to see."

When I was about twelve and my mother developed hay fever, we went to "the shore," to Rockaway, where the pollen count was low and the salt air relieved the sneezing and itching of one's eyes. We all shared one large room, my mother, sister, myself, and my father, who came for weekends. It was a cook-by-yourself place. My father would arrive on Friday around seven in the evening, pale, hot, perspired, and sooty after a two-hour ride on the Long Island Railroad. My sister and I, toasted like plump buns, greeted him at the station. Later we carried his towel and watched him dive into the crested waves.

July. I'm planning a birthday party for my husband. He will be fifty-two years old. The number of cards in a deck. Is one game complete, another about to begin? Ridiculous notion. You live with someone a long time and project your own metaphors on them. The card players were my parents, not my husband. And the legacy of the hand they dealt is mine. This upheaval—moratorium?—is mine. It is I who've lost my mother, and who've drifted away from the nothing and nowhere of the world. Yet I want very much to celebrate my husband's birthday. One of his perennial fantasies is to have a party with a fifty-piece band—in the style of the old Paul Whiteman orchestra—with a platform encircling the house for tap dancers. He's big on tap dancing.

The party will be on the twenty-first of July. I'll invite all his friends and cook a big paella with mounds of saffron rice heaped with mussels and clams and lobster from the Long Island waters. And there'll be lots of red wine.

If she were here, she'd insist on being driven to Southampton to buy gifts. Hand-tailored batiste shirts, cashmeres, Egyptian-cotton pajamas, ivory or pale blue, bright-colored Shetland sweaters—last year it was saffron-yellow, the previous year lavender. I'd protest the expense. She'd pooh-pooh my niggardliness—Bella bought gifts with queenly lavishness. This year I'm tempted to buy something on her behalf. A perverse notion? One that would serve only to sadden? I must stop myself from becoming a transmitter of sorrow. A gloom mongerer. Fear is catching. Every once in a while, I take myself silently in hand. You are a mother, a wife. You have to set the example for your own daughters. Return to your senses. What's the point of pining? Better to convey a sense of life's wholeness. Absorb your grief and grow from it. Oh, I know what one is supposed to do! Make do. Be human by rising above what seems unerringly inhuman! But there are days when I feel as vulnerable as one of those potato bugs you see patiently wending its way across a tennis court, only to be suddenly crushed by a player's sneaker.

Twilight. The hour of my ritual bicycle ride through the familiar countryside. Twilight. The bordering hour between light and darkness. To the left of the road soars a perfect orange sphere of sun; to the right, a pale moon ascending. This is the hour to come out. It is the hour when the rabbits and robins emerge to feed. When land and water birds circle above in great arcs. The evening poises in equilibrium between day and night, growth and repose. It is the hour when farmers water their crops.

Halsey Lane. Settled 1638. An old black Labrador dog trots over as he does every evening, follows me a while, and then returns home. I pedal along, legs pumping, body moving of its own accord. My back today seems stronger. The wheels vibrate underneath. The road gets consumed and left behind. I move past potato fields in pinkish-white blossom, past cornfields feather-stitched like samplers with the young green blades, past a tawny sash of earth knotted with ruby and chartreuse rosettes of lettuce, past soil crisscrossed with flaming yellow zucchini blossoms. Tilled fields wander down to wetlands and to fringes of reeds that separate land from lagoon. Long Island is horizontal,

the sort of land that convinces you the world is flat.
Long Island is cultivated. Tame. Benign. Yielding to
man's labor. Responsive to his effort. Till, and you shall
reap.

Every evening I take this ride. I did it then, while she
lived, I do it now. Evening is the bridge that spans the
world in bloom and the world of memory. Always I go
forth looking for her. But today somehow it is different.
She is with me before I set out. Her features have
merged as in a cameo and it is as if I am wearing that
cameo. I have a new sense of her. Not as an absence,
but as a staying force. I am imbued with her gaze, her
presence, her aura. I can see those prisms of light that
darted from the dark pupils of her eyes, that way she
had of holding her head. She seems to be hovering near.
Today I do not cry.

I pedal past the seventeenth-century Water Mill
cemetery with its gravestone rubbings and little sunken
stones. Old names: Halsey, Burnett, Hildreth, Sayre.
People who died at ages ripe and immature. "Phoebe
Jennings, who departed this life October 5th A.D. 1791,
in the 82nd year of her age."

The light goes violet. Shadows lengthen and turn
blue. Shadow. That blue patch where light does not hit.
Shadows which define the real. A fine dark rim borders
the sun, the moon is yellowing. My pedals move on. I
am propelled forward. The air is soft. Some sunflowers
bordering a field of rye which appeared last week like
leering pornographic blooms today seem like benign
totems, primal sunbursts.

Today I'm not pedaling fast. Not running on this
wheeling earth as if in escape or on a chase, against the
wind, breath burning in my throat, lungs searing in my

chest. Today I'm able to say: My mother's time was over. One's time comes to an end.

I see her clearer. Seeing involves focusing, paying attention; it also requires standing back, letting go. If you stand too close to an object, you cannot see it. As Yeats said: "Nothing that we love over much / Is ponderable to our touch." Today I am less frantic, straining less, cajoling less. It's as if my inner eye has opened and imprinted my mother on the retina of my soul. I see her, not in linear flashes, in broken frames, but in a steady luminous flow like a scroll endlessly unwinding. And as her image grows clearer, I am with her, filled with her, and freer to remember.

I pedal along. Am pedaled along. I breathe in the air. Light flutters over the water like a blessing and the water returns tender silvery lights of its own.

Backsliding. The notion of organizing a birthday party for my husband is abandoned. Occasions of celebration incite fresh grief. We're invited to the twenty-fifth wedding anniversary of close friends. A lawn party on a superb July night. Torches. Musicians.

First encounter: A summer acquaintance, an attractive woman of theosophist persuasion, declares how nice it is to see me. "It's been a year, hasn't it?" "Since last summer," I tell her. "And how are you?" she asks. "My mother died." "Oh, I'm so sorry, mine did too, several years ago," she says. "How did it affect you?" I ask. Her gaze, open and serene, her eyes luminous in torchlight. "My mother's death was an inspiration. Her life was perfect. She was a model of total giving."

Yes, I tell myself, wandering off. That's okay, a sound

viewpoint, applicable to Bella's death. Of course, exalt in her life, its plenitude, don't dwell on her death. She felt her mission was accomplished. Remember that rash statement she once made? "I'm a free woman," she said. And when asked to elaborate, she gazed at me in that direct way of hers and said simply, "I'm free to die. My big work is over." Yet, why does my heart pound and my stomach somersault as I turn away from the theosophist? Is her clue transferable? Or merely a remark to be shrugged off as one more platitude, a truism, an untruism, the doggerel of spiritist leanings?

Second encounter: Self-initiated. Deliberately, I seek out one particular individual amid the shadowy margin of rejoicers. Mother of the hostess. A splendid Frenchwoman in her mid-seventies whom I haven't seen since Christmas and who has come from France especially for this celebration. Animated, intelligent, a gifted musician, a warmhearted, active, brave human being. Only last Christmas she was recovering from abdominal surgery for cancer. Tonight I find her festively dressed and chatting with one of the guests. We embrace. She introduces me to her companion, we exchange civilities, he excuses himself. My friend wants to be brought up to date on everything: my work, my husband, my children. Fighting tears, I tell her. My mother died. She grasps my hands and words of commiseration pour forth in French. One dreams, counts, commiserates in one's mother tongue. My throat constricts. I've nothing else to say. *Why* did I deliberately seek out this woman to burden her? At her age, in view of her recent bout with cancer, in view of the occasion —an only daughter's silver anniversary—why bring bad news? Why trigger the natural misgivings of her own mortality? How selfish—I've tracked her down to be with my mother. I'm still searching in the crowd for my mother. But, secretly, am I perhaps also asking: How come she's here and my mother is not? How come I'm here and my mother is not?

Third encounter: A young ophthalmologist approaches me. An effusive man, a respected doctor, he knew my mother slightly, admired her and showed her considerable kindness during her brief hospital stay a few years ago. A mutual friend has apparently told him the sad news. He expresses sorrow at my loss. I nod vacantly. How did it happen, he wants to know. I provide details, then my voice breaks. There's no room now for decorum. It is urgent at times to expose our skeleton, to expose the death inside. He stands helpless, hands dangling, eyes sorrowful behind the glint of his strong lenses. "I'm so sorry I raised it . . ." he blurts out. "I didn't mean to . . ." I shake my head and feebly try to relieve his blundering litany of regrets. "It's all right," I whisper, and escape from him and the crowd, I find a wooden chair on the outskirts of the grounds overlooking a potato field. Huddled there, I give vent to tears, making no effort to muffle my sobs. The din of the merrymakers and of the music drowns out everything. But even were there a pause, my weeping could be the keening of sea gulls.

Millions of stars blink unperturbed in the deep summer sky like cold gems thrown on a jeweler's swath of velvet. Their stellar abundance, their indifferent phosphorescence infuriate me. In the distance, musicians strike up "The Anniversary Waltz" and the celebrating couple move out into the clearing to dance amid the encircling guests.

What is the point of all these words spilling forth? Words! Write about what you know, they say. This outpouring of feeling, of self-pity, is less what I know than what I have to do. It is a crying on Mama's shoulder, a wailing into the wind, a hiccuping amid sobs against an irrevocable crashing surf. A lament. A dirge. You come. And you go. I had her once, and now she's gone. So, what's new? What's the point?

I meet casual acquaintances, people I haven't seen for some time. They ask the simple question: How are you? And instead of replying with a wry, Don't ask, as she might have, my news comes tumbling forth. Like a murderer who has a need to tell about his crime. How is it possible to talk of anything else? Do you know? Have you heard? Can you tell? *It alone is true.* Why am I telling it? For sympathy? To be pitied as a small child? Only she could pity me as I wish to be pitied. *Mama sheinenkeh*, she might say, and that in itself would comfort me. Is it to let acquaintances know that I'm not the same person? Insinuating that they handle me with caution? Reassess me? What can anyone say. Or is it to assert my specialness, my special grief? Vanity, in short.

Why am I writing this?

It is less a homage, an elegy, or a requiem to her, it seems, than a barrage of my own uncontainable rantings. A gust of agitation which has swept over me, a mistral of the soul, a partial eclipse of my true self. She died. She died on me. It happens. Dead is dead. That's life. That's evolution. That's all, folks. Resign yourself. *No hay remedio. Punto final,* say the Spaniards. *S'vet gornisht helfen,* according to the Jews.

Dead and buried, my mother would say. Life has a foregone conclusion. The end. The same absurd unoriginal ending, always. Such is life's course. Life's curse.

Soon, despite the great discontinuity, you learn to live with it, like a bad knee, or a bum back. "Oh, my aching back!" you moan. "Oh, my aching life!" But then you adjust your movements, accommodate, compensate for the soreness, rise above your affliction. Life goes on. One must again take up one's duties. Pull oneself together. Keep treading water. Who knows? Perhaps death can be absorbed, even handled "creatively," "constructively"—conventionally. As my mother used to say, What's the use to complain?

But no.

I refuse to screen out the thought of her death. To dodge it. To divest myself of it. It's the only thing on my mind. Despite what I appear to be doing.

Some friends with young children visit for a long weekend. For days, I don't come to my notes. Then I feel worse. As if I'd been away from her. And unable to get to a phone when I wanted to talk to her. Have I turned these notes into a crutch? They are in fact as much of a need as a release. A way of keeping her present.

A book, any book, has to do with birth. This one, however, is a kind of dying of my old self. The end of an era. At times, tears wet my fingers. Yet, through the entries, I'm able to settle, crystallize, re-create, reconstruct, reintegrate my memories. To recall images of the past and possibly rescue her from my grief in order to possess her in lifelong union.

If only I could say it all. If only I weren't leaving out her lightness, the laughter. A *shayne gelechter*, a fine laugh, as the ironic expression goes.

Our eldest daughter comes to visit. I meet her at the station, watch from a distance as she descends the train, somewhat awkwardly, for supported under each arm is a bulky canvas. She smiles, we embrace. I ask to see the paintings; she refuses to expose their faces till we're at home. There, she hangs them. Exuberant studies, one in orange and pink, the other in green and blue.

From her minimal luggage she extracts a swathe of fabric, cerulean blue—to make me a bikini. Nothing demure. She's also brought a flask of coconut oil to anoint my back for massage, and incense to render the total accompanying environment. Her hands are strong. We breathe in unison as they move from my shoulder to neck, along the vertebrae, toward the toes. Her hands transmit energy, strength, love, well-being. Touch reduces pain. Pain in the spine. The pain of separation. Nina, our firstborn, mothers me.

And along with the love, still the old pitfalls. The chance remark that triggers unspoken, unresolved conflicts. The false note that stirs the sediment of raw feeling. That strain and resistance between mother and daughter, inevitable in the painful ongoing efforts to separate. An intense mutuality, and estrangement. An overlapping, and a gulf.

It is seemingly impossible to protect those we love from the negative things we do them. Those unwitting betrayals and rejections. Always, especially if you've not seen one another for a while, you want to say, not one thing, but everything. About love and hopes and caring. About life and death and meaning. You want to have that infinitely healing conversation in which words transcend the pain shared by mother and daughter. To share everything at last. To attain acceptance of each other, and self-acceptance. But words scutter sideways and miss the object. Secrets hide in the interstices of language. Conversations end in silence.

When my daughter leaves, we hold each other lovingly, and release each other lovingly. Her visit heals. She brings me closer to my mother and my past. As St. Theresa said, "I have no defense against affection."

Memories of motherhood.

An infant, eyes still shut from the glare of the world, hands fluttering at random, mouth rooting instinctively for the breast. A phantom smile flitting across the child's face as her tongue plays with the nipple. The body going soft and limp after nursing. I raise her to my shoulder, noting again those faint red markings beneath the translucent skin at the nape of the neck where the blood vessels are transparent. Stork's beak, as it's designated in folklore.

The shadows of an infant's legs upon the wall as her limbs move in the dark.

The touch of firm, warm flesh when you lift an infant in the middle of the night, damp with perspiration, urine, the exertion of sleep.

The pressure of a child's arm encircling your neck when you take her from the high chair.

The lathering of her body in the bath.

The tacit coordination between mother and child as a small arm extends into a sleeve, or a leg into a pajama.

That ineffable instant when a child's face raises

toward yours to impart a moist, mouth-to-mouth good-night kiss.

The grand soliloquy when the lights are out and the child, upright in bed, addresses the vague shapes of toys and shadows, gesticulating and dramatizing, transported like Don Quixote in his discourse on the Golden Age. The elderly knight had his imaginary creatures and vision, the child has hers.

I remember motherhood, I remember my childhood.

M y dreams are changing. Two nights in a row I see my mother, not in everyday acts of life, but lying in bed, her hair white, propped against pillows, eyes vulnerable, strength ebbing. I see her in those last days. Moving toward her end. In dreams, the death scene is reenacted.

One Sunday morning I'm awakened from one of those dreams by a horde of migrating wild geese. A frantic honking overhead like a police squadron racing toward a crime. For several moments it goes on, this wild flapping, this aerial shuffle of wings, this agitation, this tailgating pursuit in flight. At a certain moment the honking changes and turns into an outcry, like a troop of Arab women shrieking, a high-pitched cacophony, the sound of fear, of primitive maternal wails.

How many stations in our lives? Three? Birth, Growth, Death? Or five? Birth; Weaning, number one (from the breast); Weaning, number two (adolescence); Weaning, number three (decease of the parents); and Death.

The rush of birds ceases. Stillness. I have no one but myself. The departed child in myself, and her migration.

Pain is a lonely thing. When it comes, it is yours alone. You hunger for solitude.

Sitting at a distance from the house, where the soil is soft with the humus of last year's leaves, I observe the burrow of a mole, follow the underground progress of that small creature as it tunnels in pilgrimage toward earth's true center.

Kneeling in a miniature flower bed of periwinkles, forget-me-nots, pinks, pansies, and verbena, their small petals beaded and sharply colored after a rain, I pick off dead blooms.

Wandering off in the afternoon to a hidden stream where watercress grows. The water, icy and dark, coils like a ribbon through hazy woods of young oak. Here and there, the gleam of eddies. Floating downstream, fragments of moldering wood, a random scarlet leaf, the orange cupola of a jewelweed blossom. Clumps of glossy watercress rise in jungle exuberance from the soft sandy bottom. Fragile miniature plantlets, thickly seeded, bob on the limpid surface. The vista downstream is deep and endless and green. A world growing green. Recalling García Lorca's "Somnambular Ballad" for a departed beloved one: *Verde que te quiero verde / Verde viento, verdes ramas* . . . Green, how I want you green / Green wind / Green boughs . . .

Down to the sea. Lying on the sand alone, filmed with brine. The deserted beach ruffled in kelp and meerschaum. Bubbles of organic matter quivering and bursting under shafts of primordial light. Blue-black mussels clinging to earth's torso of rock against the rush of green surf. Sandpipers tracking footprints on the ancient ridged yellow sand—twilight hieroglyphics. Insatiable gulls haggling and shrieking like fish peddlers over the shifting sea. Scattered clouds hurrying east. The sun, yellow as the yolk of unborn eggs, sails west, casting splinters of gold upon the water. The dune grass stirs. Everything is in motion.

Caught in my bathing suit I find a tiny seashell, and inside it the fragment of a crab's carcass. I pick it out, lay it on the sand, this prehistoric remnant, a survival of a bygone era. Inert.

I lie on the towel, on the sand, on the world. Alone. Longing for that which has been lost, which there is no hope of ever possessing again. It is the way. The endless chain. I gaze out toward the water for its comfort and answers. Water that stirs memories. Water, salt, saline tears. Pools of dark float amid crests of light. A scarlet ribbon of sun binds the horizon of earth to infinity. I stretch out on the sand and close my eyes. Bursts of light explode behind my eyelids and the warmth of the sand invades my body.

Am I healing? I'm able to gaze at her photograph without that tourniquet tightening round my throat, clamping memory. Without hot tears flooding my eyes. Tears that blur the image, obliterate the past. When you try so hard to trace every feature, the profile inevitably gets lost. I find myself now able to look at that close-up of her and to discern the jolly glint, the animated stance, the practical gaze, the calm look. I can find comfort, not merely agony. I need to look at her picture less, and I see more. I'm beginning to see her in *her* life, and not only myself bereft of her life. I can hear her saying with a little smile: *Enough. Don't cry. Be a mensh! You have your life ahead of you.* Who was it that said: A mother is not to lean on, but to make leaning unnecessary?

I remember so many things.

As a child, I'd sit on the edge of the tub on an evening when she was going out, watch her comb her hair and with her forefinger dab a bit of color on her lips. How good she smelled.

I remember how she straightened her dress, gripping its sides and giving a smart downward pull.

I remember her warming a bit of olive oil and rubbing it on my scalp with a ball of cotton to give sheen to my hair.

I remember how she'd encourage me, when nauseous, to stick two fingers into my mouth to vomit.

I remember when I had my tonsils out, awakening from the ether in a white iron hospital bed with bars at its side, my throat raw like an uprooted organ—and five teeth missing. The doctor had decided, while he had me under ether, to remove the loose baby teeth. My tongue slipped over the empty gaps. I felt doubly castrated. My mother cheered me. "Lucky girl, rid of your tonsils and ready for new teeth." She brought me vanilla ice cream.

I remember her pinching me in pique. Once she remarked that the shortest route away from trouble in the head is via the backside.

I remember her hemming my long yellow dotted-swiss prom dress. By eye. Making it uneven all the time, till that ankle-length gown wound up midi-length.

I remember her perennial question, "How can you sew without a thimble?"

I remember her sureness in selecting fresh vegetables in the market.

I remember how she sliced vegetables into soup, or salad. Every which way, and never on a cutting board, her thumb the prop.

I remember her separating the yolk and white of an egg: one smart crack of the shell against a dish, two quick gyrations of the wrist, release of the white into one saucer, and the plop of the yolk into another.

I remember her rolling dumplings into soup, moistening fingers and palms in a cup of water between each dumpling so they wouldn't stick.

I remember her cutting noodles, kneading dough, puffing pillows.

I remember her reaching for a pinch of kosher salt from the white enamel saltbox marked in black old-fashioned letters, and the creak of the crystals when released into the pot.

I remember her heating the thick salt in a skillet and filling a long sock with it to apply on my cheek for toothache.

I remember the rush of hot milk boiling over as she fixed a hot drink sweetened with honey for my bronchial cough. For some reason, the skim that formed repulsed me; she always removed it.

I remember her laying mustard plasters on my chest, and setting a steaming kettle before me, a towel tenting my head, to inhale the vapors and relieve the congestion.

I remember her wringing out socks from soapy water and hanging them on the bathroom dryer, which she pulled up and down from the ceiling on a squeaky pulley.

I remember her twinkling expression when my sister

and I, teenagers, sallied forth from the house on a double date, decked out in black fishnet hose and puffing, à la George Sand, on little white-enamel pipes.

I remember her bathing our infants in their early days. After the bath, she'd lay the languorous baby on the Bathinette, dust the body with talc, knead and tuck the young flesh. Faint gurgling sounds emerged from the infant, rosy and groggy with heat. On went the pajamas with birds and animals and padded feet; tops got snapped to bottoms. The infant's damp fleecy hair was brushed. Then Bella would settle on the rocking chair, the fragrant child sprawled on her lap, content as a cat in a fish store, guzzling a bottle of warm milk.

I remember how she overwatered our plants in summer.

I remember her voice, its inflections and rhythms, as she talked about her home in Poland.

I remember calling up to the sixth floor, "Mama, throw me down a nickel." Confident that no matter where she was, she'd hear me.

Summer is ending. Late golden August days in plenitude, like peaches overripe and bursting from their skins. Roses unfurl amid dizzying perfumes. Trumpet vines have gone berserk. The pungency of tomatoes and basil sends you flying for garlic and olive oil. End of summer. Sarah and I sit on the wooden-slat chairs overlooking the bay. Our eyes follow the course of herons and gulls plummeting white toward the water. A flock of Canadian geese circles overhead. They swoop and ascend, move southward in V-formation, then, obeying some inner cue, wheel around in unison and drive in the opposite direction. Recovering space past. Is it not time yet for them to go? Soon comes our turn for migration. Time for the city, work, school, elevators, subways, urban everydayness. We sit quietly, my youngest daughter and I, absorbing summer's sounds and scents. It is that hour when you want to be still and listen to the birdcalls of the loon and the phoebes and inhale the heady fragrance of nicotiana, which yields its perfume only in late afternoon. Oh, how often Bella sat here in spacious silence, gazing out at the iridescent bay, at the shadows of trees lengthening and darkening on the other shore, their trunks reflected like great roots in the water. As if reading my thoughts, Sarah abandons her chair and comes and sits in my lap. It's years since she's done that. "Oh, Mommy, I keep thinking of Bella. All the time. I miss her so much. You know?" My lips compress, my eyes brim. I nod. Sarah leans against me. This beautiful young woman of sixteen summers, her hair streaked golden by salt and sun, her flesh tanned, firm, and strong. I stroke her hair, in this ineffable moment when the two of us, occupying Bella's chair, poise in primal closeness. She buries her head against me. "Oh, I don't want you and Daddy to die!" August plenitude. A child's onset of dread. Parents one day age and die.

A new bicycle. Ten-speed. My first ride on the new steed. The rusty twenty-year-old English Rudge idles in the shed. Having made the run so often, it was like an old nag on whom the rider could drop the reins and allow it to pick its way unheeded down familiar Halsey Lane. My body leans forward tentatively over the unaccustomed tilt of the handlebars on the new apparatus. Timidly, I begin tinkering with the gears, pulling the lever toward me as I go uphill. The aim, the salesman told me, is to maintain a steady pedaling. To keep your legs in regular motion. I pedal along.

The twilight ride, again. Autumn approaching. Cornfields lush and heavy with tasseled ears. Huge sunflowers lined up like sentinels before meadows of swaying rye. Roadside asters, goldenrod, Queen Anne's lace. Pink mallows by the water and ripened beach plums. Laden potato trucks, gleaners in the fields. A single eggplant dropped from a harvester's load lies on the dusty road. Further on, a rabbit flayed by passing wheels. I pedal on. Again, thinking of her.

My mother let go. I let her go. Yet always I am carrying her in me. Even find myself picking up some of her habits. This eternal attachment. Women—mothers. Daughters—mothers. The daughter leaves the mother. Separation, that essential task of adolescence, attended at times by anger, rebellions, rejections. Then rapprochement. Finally, the ultimate separation, the inevitable task of adulthood. Accompanied by numbness, hurt, anger. And then . . . what?

I pedal along. Seventeenth-century clapboard houses nestle behind sprawling apple trees. From somewhere an invisible apple thumps to the ground. The end. Like an invisible life. How does an individual perceive his end? On that last day of her life, on that last afternoon, she made a fresh bequest. Heedful still of her survivors. Of futurity. A bequest for one of her grandchildren. At the time, I glossed over it, consenting readily, and spoke of other things. Of course, she knew then that she was dying. But how easy she made it for us. Was it easy for her?

In the last few days, I am less agitated. Lonely, longing, but less agitated. I've stopped circling through the days as if in a revolving door. I feel myself pruned back to the mother stem. Like those vines that we saw in the Galician countryside outside Santiago de Compostela. At harvest end, the vines were pruned back to their origin. Strength and survival endure in the roots.

Since my mother's death I've been holding on, clinging desperately to her and to a youthful version of myself. Losing her physical being, her force, her umbrage, seemed a maiming, even an annihilation, of my own existence. She was the *mysterium tremendum* of life.

But that season is over.

Slowly I find myself being weaned from her material presence. Yet, filled with her as never before. It is I now who represent us both. I am our mutual past. I am my mother and my self. She gave me love, to love myself, and to love the world. I must remember how to love.

Piece by piece, I reenter the world. A new phase. A new body, a new voice. Birds console me by flying, trees by growing, dogs by the warm patch they leave behind on the sofa. Unknown people merely by performing their motions. It's like a slow recovery from a sickness, this recovery of one's self. The old self, that bustling, jaunty, smiling, compliant version, turns the corner and vanishes. Gone is that pinch-penny effort to accordion each calendar day. Time is a gift rather than a goad. Diminished is concern about people's opinions, abandoned the notion of perfection, the illusion that children can be spared grief and disappointment.

I knew a beautiful woman once. And she was my

mother. I knew a tenderness once. And it was my mother's. Oh, how happy I was to be loved.

And now I mourn her. I mourn that cornerstone. I mourn her caring. I mourn the one who always hoped for me. I mourn her lost image of me. The lost infant in myself. My lost happiness. I mourn my own eventual death. My life now is only mine.

She was the one who taught me to love and to receive love. To be unafraid. In her life and in the way she met death. My mother was at peace. She was ready. A free woman. "Let me go," she said. Okay, Mama, I'm letting you go.

The time has come to separate. For me to go back to the world alone.

I loved you till you were gone and now even more. Every blade, every leaf, every seed in my portion of the world has shifted. Your presence hovers everywhere, over house, over garden, over dreams, over silence. You are within me. I'll not lose you.

Once I was born. Can I be born again? Oh, wean me from pain to love. Help me to use your love and strength in my own life. Help me to carry my world.

It is time to reshuffle the deck for a new game. To re-create my world, reassemble the pieces, weed the garden, pick the apples, fill the vases, finish reading the passage I fell asleep on last night.

The road winds home. I open our front door. A yeasty smell drifts forth from the kitchen. I stand on the threshold. Sarah looks up from the kitchen table, her hands webbed with sticky dough. "Guess what?" She smiles. "I'm baking bread. Today's the first time. Look, I've poured the flour, made a well, added the yeast and everything else. Tell me, Mommy, how long do you have to knead?"

I walk over, stand by her, and hear myself echoing old words, reenacting an ancient legend: "It isn't a matter of time. You knead till it feels right."